Tragic Hero

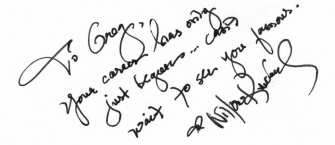

Tragic Hero

A Teacher Accused

Willow Kincaid

To order additional copies of this book, contact:
Xlibris Corporation
1-888-795-4274
www.Xlibris.com
Orders@Xlibris.com
38730

Contents

This book is dedicated

to a Sicilian child, who has tolerated generations of nebulous origin and still loved me enough to save my life

~ACKNOWLEDGMENTS~

Thank you to:

Amiee Mann for writing the line that personifies my eldest child,
Kurt Cobain and Nirvana for providing a panacea from the Prince,
Tilda Mae for her crotchety advice bestowed through her granddaughter,
The lady who made winter realization possible in the summer,

AND

One of the "M's:" the original ex-student-who-became-my-friend,
The life-saving code words from the son of Odin,
The unconditional love of my NC girl,
All the NOMADS . . .

AND especially

That little girl with the red velvet lampshade

BUT, once and forever
One of the few who has ever truly confounded me:
"Tell me something we both know . . . to prove it's really you."
"Euthanasia."
 . . . you'll always be in my heart . . .

INTRODUCTION/ DISCLAIMER/PROLOGUE

Read This

(I know you like to skip this introduction/prologue/disclaimer section,
but, in this case, you can't.)

This is a true story about a high school teacher who was accused of an inappropriate relationship with a student. The names of any and every thing which could reveal an identity have been changed for the obvious reasons. What you have in your hands at this moment is Part One of the three part tale. It wasn't my plan to write it as a trilogy, it was more like it wrote itself that way. I started putting it on paper in the first place because during my very first year of teaching (different school), a lunatic student began stalking me and it was ultimately my detailed notes on his various actions that yielded corrective action. The three parts of this tale probably happened somewhat relative to very definite phases—physical and emotional. My . . . or rather . . . our story is so bizarre and incredible I believe time (I'll amend this credit later) actually intervened, dividing the painful process in a manner which, frankly, kept me from killing myself.

So, I'm telling you upfront with what you are involving yourself, if you are about to start reading this book.

First of all, (don't you hate when people say something like "First of all?" or like, "Number 1?" makes you worry that some boring shit is going to go on forever. Well, don't worry. I totally hear you on that, and I will try to be concise even though you will find if you continue to read, that brevity is not my strong suit. Believe me, sorting out and organizing all that is relative to your and **my** understanding of the events has been similar to searching for a thousand diamond chips in the gargantuan dumpster of a busy restaurant. Now you see what I mean about my issues with "brevity"?)

Okay, here is how it goes. There are currently only four people breathing on the planet who know the precise truth about what happened. You could add yourself to this list if you are smart, but you will have to read all three parts of this story. The part of which you are now in possession is basically a factual narrative of the period encompassing the cold day it all started until roughly the beginning of spring. Following the directive you are reading now is a section of background. In fact there is pertinent background information scattered throughout the pages. If you aspire to ferret out the truth on your own and get yourself added to the current list of four, you need to realize that nothing included in any of the three books is there by accident.

To explain the way this speculative, non-fictional tale begins would undermine your intelligence, so I can't give you much direction. All I will say is that the mysterious aspect of our entire story is only mysterious to a percentage of the population I like to call the 95%. (You will be intimately familiar with this percentage if you traverse the complete three part journey.) What I suppose matters to me (to us) is whether you are able to answer in the affirmative the questions below. If you hesitate to respond "yes" to any of them, I suggest you return this loaned copy from your friend or borrowed copy from the library or stolen copy from a park bench back to from whence it came and watch television instead.

Ask yourself now:

f.   are you able to keep your mind open to ideas as yet unfathomed?
d.   can you pay attention to detail as minute as it may be?

q. are you willing to reserve judgment until you have pondered all evidence?

z. do you understand the time-consuming task of "pondering"?

Wait. More than anything else, I want you to ask yourself if you really and truly know/feel/understand what love is.

That is the beginning . . .

BACKGROUND

AIDAN TALKS TO GOD

I promise I'm not starting on the day I was born and telling my whole life story. If you knew any of the 900+ students I taught in my relatively short stint, they would tell you I am not a lecturer. I'd always much rather we were doing something in the classroom. Okay, since some of you readers probably **are** my ex-students, I am acknowledging that I didn't say I didn't "talk." That statement might qualify as the first contribution to one of the problems with my methodology, I suppose—the fact that I might not lecture, but I would talk about pretty much anything. I'll just let you be the ultimate judge of any wrongdoing.

Actually, if I did recount my life story you would undoubtedly be entertained, but that would not be as a result of some glamorous, enviable lifestyle—quite the contrary; you would be entertained only because: a) I am an engaging storyteller with a sharp sense of humor and b) the more time elapsed between tragedy and the telling of it, the easier it is to convert it to comedy. Now what is so perplexing to me is that second part because I swear to you, as much as I believe that time lessens the intensity of events and heals what had seemed broken forever, I cannot, **cannot** imagine applying that remedy to what has happened over the last ten months. Over my entire stretch on earth, I can recall excruciating emotional pain, paralyzing desperation, loss so irreparable I cried every day for over a year, and the crushing disillusionment of false love over and over and . . . , but this? *My FO*? I have no words light years within reach to explain how it has affected me.

None of that is the issue at hand. Come to think about it, what I need to promise is not to give you too much background but to try and contain my tangent rants. Stream of consciousness is so confusing unless the reader is also the writer, so I promise to **try** to keep the segues to a minimum. Since I'm imparting this useful information months after I began journaling what has become *Tragic Hero*, I doubt I will edit out any ramblings already down, but you could get lucky. A prince, I know, has signed on to do some of the typing, and, though equally as verbose as I, he has almost zero tolerance for extraneous bullshit. It is safe to say I will probably defer to him, and if you take on the entire trilogy, you will defer to him as well—in the end.

But—background is background, and you won't get a fair try at joining the four if I withhold relative information, so . . .

April 30, 1989

I went to church. My five year old son, Aidan, stayed home with a babysitter. The sermon that day focused on whether or not the devout of the congregation had ever seen god. (Sorry, no capital letter. It's personal.) At lunch I asked Aidan if he had ever seen god. Without hesitation and matter-of-factly he responded that he'd never seen god, but he HAD talked to him once. I was both amused and intrigued, which I had grown accustomed to with this child.

I asked, "Really? What did he say?"

Aidan chewed his sandwich exaggeratedly which felt patronizing to me. "I asked him to make Cletus," he finally answered.

Now I was confused, or rather, I thought my son was. This Cletus person is my youngest brother who was at least 20 years old when Aidan was born.

I smiled indulgently at my little lunatic. "Honey, you do know that Uncle Cletus was born a long time before you were."

My son swallowed his mouthful and explained as if I was a deaf non-English speaker. "It was when I was **with** god that I asked him to make Cletus."

I had no words, and, although I recall a frosty layer crawling over my skin at that moment, it wasn't until a few days later when realization struck and forever engraved itself on my consciousness.

May 3, 1989

I had a hard time being a stay-at-home mom. It wasn't that I couldn't find a trillion things by which to entertain myself, it was finding common ground with a five year old (who rarely slept, by the way). So, I met other stay-at-home-moms, arranged "play dates" for our children, signed Aidan up with the local ankle biter sports' leagues and dropped him off at pre-school from 1-3 on weekdays. In retrospect I can see how we all would have been so much better off if I had engaged in some meaningful work at that time. Yes, yes, I know, raising children is the most meaningful . . . rewarding . . . valuable . . . worthwhile . . . blah, blah, blah . . . ingrained patriarchal propaganda conveniently killing two potential rebellions with one arrow to the heart. (I'm teetering at the edge of one of my favorite tirades and tearing myself away with superhuman strength). I feel the alienation of some readers seeping through the pages as my intense vibrations begin to emanate outward screaming the number one impediment on my list of obstacles to evolution—the patriarchy. How the hell did we let that happen?)

Just for one second let me speak, because the prince will want to challenge and rile me. He finds my passion comical. (Note to self: Don't let him type this part.) Does anyone, even a good portion of the 95 need evidence to support what the primary ideology of the patriarchy is? (Okay, my citing textual references will only garner allegiance from those already pledged. Let me whip out a few scenarios relative to the masses.) If you want to understand how our culture is regressing, just check a few statistics on the number of women CEOs or female billionaires. Fill out a form for a variety of companies through their websites, and notice how many require a title before you may continue to page two. A title, you know, "Mr., Mrs., Miss, Ms." Now why should that be a required field? What necessary information does the company obtain? Whether you are male or female? (er, . . . discrimination.) Whether you are a married or single female? The company must not be concerned with the marital status of males since "Mr." is a one-size-fits-all-men title. And what of "Ms.," in the progressive 2000's? In the era of women's rights (light years ago in the 1970's) "Ms." offered women, who didn't think their marital status was anyone's cause for consideration, a neutral option. What is the current interpretation of "Ms."? All you 5%-ers who abhor free-floating information probably accepted, adopted and were done at the initial explanation, but let me tell you what I have heard from our precious borderline adults. In a word association format "Ms." (for the majority of the classroom) brings up "feminist." So, I ask, "What does it mean to be a feminist?" Here comes the proof of de-evolution. Someone, anyone, everyone answers, "Means you're a lesbian." Too many nods of agreement, every year, every class and let me not forget to add that the word "lesbian" is generally uttered as if the student suddenly has permission to swear. One more time, one more day, morning, minute, one more inhale and I will slit my throat just to never again hear the pathetic apathy forming syllables of such ignorant ingratitude for the past sacrifices now taken for granted. Beyond "taken for granted," they are literally disparaged. I want to cry. (I am this second heading back to May 3rd; the prince will respect my ire and syntax, but we'll all agree that was a monstrous tangent.)

One of Aidan's and my joint activities was shopping, (primarily for shit nobody needs), but along the mall route are always bookstores. On that particular day I was perusing racks of texts relative to spirit or inspiration or psychology or possibly inspirational psychology of the spirit, when a book suddenly stared at me. I don't remember the exact title, but large enough on the cover were the words, "near-death experiences of children." The subject reflected my specific interests in no discernible manner at the time, so I don't know why I was compelled to pick it up. As was my usual habit when I had no author or genre in mind, I opened the book to a random page. (This habit has generally served me well in deciding whether or not these haphazard picks can hold my interest or are worth my time.) The following is what I began to read and is the shortest version of which I am capable.

> A nine-year-old girl had been in a coma for a few weeks. On this day her parents were down the hall, and a nurse was the only other person in the room. Suddenly the girl opened her eyes, looked around the room and clearly demanded, "Where are Jeff and Billy?" Of course, the nurse got very excited, and after a quick attempt to placate the girl, she rushed off to locate the parents.

The nurse related the good news to the ecstatic parents, and, assuming Jeff and Billy to be names of recognizable playmates, she forewarned the parents of their daughter's quite determined desire to see them. As the parents flew to their child's room, they hurriedly questioned each other concerning the identity of the two—each believing that the other would know. By the time they reached the bedside, both parents were bewildered about the issue of Jeff and Billy, but they were too overjoyed at their daughter's return to pursue the matter.

A few weeks later the author of the book interviewed the little girl, and he brought up the subject. He asked if she remembered the names or that they were the first people she had asked for upon "waking up." The interviewer also mentioned that neither of her parents seemed to know any of her friends by those names.

"So, do you remember this?" He asked her, "Do you know who Jeff and Billy are?"

She responded without hesitation, "Oh, yes, they were souls waiting to be born."

I anticipate the reader understanding my reason for relating this vignette, but I'll clarify just in case my assumption is actually just my own synapse-hopping impulse. At the conclusion of the passage, my instantaneous thought was that my child, Aidan, had asked god to create my brother, Cletus, while he (Aidan) was a "soul waiting to be born." (Again, the icy wave came.)

I wish I could remember any further details Aidan might have provided on the day he explained his "talk with god" to me. I'm sure I probably did ask him for more; I can only imagine nothing more fascinating surfaced (or Aidan lost interest in the topic), since what I related of April 30th is all I had written in the notebook I kept at the time.

After I read those few pages in the book, I wondered quite a lot more. (I refrain from including all the quotation marks which would be necessary to designate the variety in connotation of the terms. I don't think you want all that interference any more than I want the labor.) Was Cletus also a soul waiting at the same time? Did Aidan know him and want to continue a relationship with him after incarnation? Did Aidan specify an uncle to god? If not, why was Cletus incarnated first? Why twenty years before Aidan? Sigh.

Here, finally, is the very fitting conclusion to this perplexing tale—note the word "conclusion" not "solution." The fact is Aidan was my mother's first grandchild. I am the second eldest of her five children, and Cletus is the baby, born about six years after

I was. When Aidan arrived Cletus was the first of my siblings to visit him, and from the minute Cletus held that baby, it seemed as though an instant familiarity appeared. My mother and I both clandestinely commented on the obvious connection between them. (You will note this apparent familiarity occurred in 1983.) As I stated previously, Cletus was about 20 years old at the time, with no children of his own, yet his manner with Aidan was so casual and easy a stranger could assume they were father and son without another thought. It was actually my brother's habit of speaking to Aidan as if he were an adult which guided my own adoption of such a practice with all my children.

Aidan is now 22, and the strength of his relationship with his uncle is more hardcore than ever. Below is a note I left for Aidan following his return from visiting Cletus in NYC, as he was about to return to his boarding high school.

Hey, baby,

SO MUCH!!

I will miss you _so_ much. I can hardly imagine you not being here. I called E— He said, and I quote, "it was great for me to see Aidan. He's such a great person to talk to."

Keep up the good work, my love. Please show before you go back. I have faith that you will find more important methods to assert your independence. ♥

—I love you,
Mom.

Notes between Aidan and Willow

I will miss you, while I'm gone too.
Here then you know, I miss you now.
Have a good day @ school. I
♡ you.

♡ Aidan

PS

I need Directions to School.

Aidan -
    Print the directions from the
M____ School website and I'll go over
them with you tonight.
    Also, if you have time, will you
make them fish? (I'll be your best friend)
Have a great day. Call if you
need anything.
        I love you like crazy.
                ♡ Mom

I ♡ you Mom, have a good 1st day.
It won't Be BAD, you got your
own room, A schedule w/ M___
Don't work too HARD. I'll
call and let you know when I
get OFF WORK, or I'll write
my schedule down before I leave.

♡ Aidan ✱

— I love you! Have a good day. I
hope work goes how you want it to.
♡ Mom

PS. Thanks for the note.

I work 4:30 → 8:00 pm MON.   D___ IS
going to pick
me up.

CALL A___ / TALK D___.   I will
still come
home

Also mom, see if you could
drive me on WED.
4:30 OR 5:00 PM
I have ALL THE INFO.

Aidan,

There's chicken in the refrigerator ...

We made a new Sim family, but V_____ neglected to put in a fire alarm (or the phone) so the dad died right away. It was sad.

I love you.

Mom

PROM PICTURES

Good evening, my son,

I hope you had fun. I am very proud of you for the way you handled you party last night. I feel strongly that I can trust you to be honest with me and that is so important.

This sounds corny, but you are like a gem to me. You're just about the most valuable thing I have in my life. I hope I treat you right.

All my love,
J

your the BEST mother in the world, I mean that.

Aidan

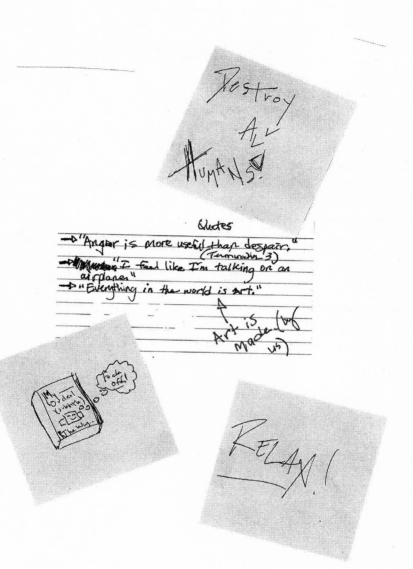

AT SCHOOL

W

On a Friday in December, at the start of the last class period of the day, Dr. Pepper Grand, the school principal, ducked her head into the English workroom and asked me if I had a minute to go and talk with her in the main office.

Of course.

I met with her and M. Lucifer, one of the assistant principals, in the relatively spacious conference room across from the principal's office. Lucifer carefully closed the door behind the three of us. The only other time I'd ever been in that room with the door closed was during a department chair meeting, (I was hired as the English chair over the previous summer.) and throughout that meeting various people kept opening the door in attempts to encourage circulation. I had been under the impression that the stifling condition of my previous experience was related to the over-capacity number of adults crowded around the table; apparently it was just a stuffy room by nature because I wished for a fan the moment I took a seat.

There was no preamble. Dr. Grand just started rolling it out.

"Willow, the reason I asked you to come down here is because we had to address an incident with a student today, and during the course of a search of his belongings we found some disturbing items that involve you."

I waited expectantly. Over the course of my six years at the school, there had been numerous instances in which I was questioned concerning my teaching methods and/or approaches to students.

Dr. Grand continued, "Willow, Caine Blaise was sent down here from In-School-Restriction today because he possessed drug paraphernalia. When Mr. Lucifer searched Caine's jacket he discovered this note . . . ," she pursed her lips while she pushed an 8 and a half by 11 photocopy of a piece of notebook paper across the table, positioning it squarely in front of me, " . . . which looks like it's in your handwriting," she finished slowly, fixing a somber gaze on my face. I didn't have to read it. In half a cursory sweep of the page, I was speechless. The words were:

> *I think we should see how many days in a row we can have sex . . . and how many times each day . . . and how many different ways. See you tonight.*

♥

My mind was going 1000 mph. I tried to remain expressionless as I frantically searched my brain for some rationale I thought they would find acceptable.

Dr. Grand's face was that of a visitor at the Holocaust museum. One arm was stretched over the conference-sized table, and she fingered the edge of the offending paper gingerly as she asked soberly, "Willow, did you write this note?"

I was a primitive robot. "No," I answered.

At my response Mr. Lucifer boisterously joined in, "You know it will be easy to find out." He was staring at me defiantly, "We can easily compare it to other things you've written."

I could almost see the ice descending like a stalactite curtain between me and M. Lucifer. No love had ever been lost between the two of us since the day he joined the administration. "I didn't write it," I said.

Lucifer leaned toward me, producing an open flip cell phone in one hand. "Well, how about this?" he hissed, apparently reading a text message, "'Morning baby . . . ,' did you send that message to Caine?"

I choked, swallowed, answered, "I sent the part about giving an SOL and bringing work to ISR," I stared right in to his hyperthyroid eyes, "but I didn't send that first part."

The bug eyes rolled, "Are you kidding me? You're saying you wrote everything but 'Morning, baby?'"

That morning was fluttering in a cloud before me.

"Yes," I replied.

"Oh my god," he huffed dramatically, looking to Dr. Grand for acknowledgement of my lunacy.

Dr. Grand sighed gravely, holding Mr. Lucifer's gaze only barely. "Willow, . . . ," she began again.

(At that point I had no idea how seriously destroyed my life was about to become. I was shocked at the presentation, but I thought I would get the chance to explain. Yes, they wanted an explanation right then, but I couldn't give it then, I needed permission.)

She kept saying my name, and I recalled from my Master's classes in Educational Administration that using a person's name is supposed to make him or her feel more comfortable. The knowledge made the ploy feel patronizing, and I felt sorry for Dr. Grand. She looked so serious and sad. I did want to dispel her angst, but I couldn't do it then and there. I didn't know that I would never get another chance.

"Willow," her heavily-lidded eyes were steady liquid reflecting me, begging me, "If there's something I need to know, please tell me now."

"No," is what I said, but what I thought was, "What you **want** me to tell you I cannot."

Pepper Grand was silent for long seconds. She fingered the note, at a dejected loss. Finally, with glassy, devastated eyes she met the eager gaze of M. Lucifer.

"Mr. Lucifer, would you ask Mr. Fangboner to come in."

M. appeared reluctant to go. I got the sense he thought he might miss something exciting but in that way people only want to be part of something out of the ordinary so they can use the knowledge to feel superior to others.

Pepper did not speak to me or look at me while we were alone.

Marshall Fangboner strode into the room with the air of handling a type of business which is regular and customary. He thrust a piece of paper in front of me while he introduced himself as a representative of human resources for the school system. He told me to read the paper carefully before I signed it as he proceeded to pretty much read it to me. I hate when people do that. Do they not trust that you'll actually read it? Do they think that even if you do read it, you won't understand it or miss the most important parts? Or maybe they just can't wait for you to get the news? (This could only matter if the information is extremely good or bad.) Or they just like to hear themselves talk. Well, none of these explanations are positive justifications anyway.

Mr. Fangboner explained to me that I was being suspended from my job (with pay) pending an investigation of what appeared to be improper conduct. For the duration of the suspension, I was not allowed to set foot on any part of my school's property.

I felt numb. I signed the paper. Fangboner excused himself to make a copy, but when he opened the door one of the other assistant principals was nearby, so Dr. Grand asked her to do it. It was about 40 minutes until the end of the school day. I asked Pepper if I could just leave now. She said, "Sure," with the most enthusiasm I'd seen displayed since back at the turn of the century when she had stepped into the English workroom, asked if she could speak to me and, in the process, changed every single aspect of my life forever.

I folded my copy carefully and went to the workroom. There were two or three teachers standing, talking, drinking coffee and smiling as if it was a normal TGIF Friday. I don't remember who they were, yet I had known them forever. I didn't speak a word, just started putting random belongings into my school bag. I felt distraught and incredulous, gathering ex-students' sample papers and projects as if I were never to return but simultaneously taking my AP kids' recent papers which needed grading. The next second I felt as if the whole thing wasn't real, so I did not take my favorite books or years of lesson plans.

I drove home quickly. It was cold outside. I had no idea what to do. My cell phone played a melody as I walked in my front door. It was a text message from my son, Aidan. It read: "Deny everything."

C

I was sitting in ISR once again. The scenario was so familiar already this year that it was like playing a game for the hundredth time just to keep your little sister from whining. No one in In-school Restriction has any vested interest toward the accomplishment of anything, they all just go through the routine while trying to find ways within the confines to stay entertained or at least look awake.

It was a Friday so I was even less serious than every other day, and truthfully I hadn't really been even close to serious about anything school-related since around 6th or 7th grade. Well, it was before lunch I know that, and I was scrolling through my phone's address book for the most promising green's keeper when this kid in one of the desks by the wall tosses a note toward me. It missed my desk, falling instead next to my foot. First thing—I shot a look at the ISR teacher, but she was turned away from me, helping some dumb ass at the computer.

Basically the note said that the kid had weed but nothing to smoke it with. He wanted to know if I had anything. Even if I hadn't, I wasn't about to let this opportunity escape. I wrote, "Yeah," and something about after school. Then I threw the wad of paper back at him.

A little later he went to the trashcan and shoved the paper under some other crap.

It was one of those suck-up-asshole types who told the ISR teacher to pick the note out of the trash. It all went down pretty fast after that.

I was sent to the main office where two of the APs, Mr. Lucifer and Mr. Marcus told me to empty my pockets. I had on my leather jacket so that's where I went first. There wasn't much of a way around it. The paraphernalia ended up on the desk.

Both administrators were acting real bad ass. Marcus could at least pull it off to a degree 'cause he was about 6 feet and pretty built, but the other guy, Lucifer, was just a joke—one of those pansy shit heads trying to make up for his shrimpy size by barking out orders at people already at a disadvantage; in this case, that would be me. Lucifer seemed less interested in the smoking devices than in getting me to produce more.

"Pant's pockets," he said, staring at me with his bug eyes.

I pulled out my phone. He held out his hand. I put the phone on the desk.

"Come on," he motioned with his finger. I started to wonder if he was looking for something in particular.

From my other pocket I pulled my wallet and a piece of computer paper which was folded several times. Lucifer unfolded the paper and read the words. Fuck, here we go. I watched his pop-eyes race back and forth over the lines. It took him less than ten seconds before he held it out in front of me.

"Who wrote this?" He asked brusquely.

I didn't answer.

He turned the writing back towards himself and shook his head, "'Cause gosh, it looks pretty familiar to me," he spoke dramatically.

He asked me again, "Who wrote this?"

I just stared at his face, thinking how much it would suck to be him.

Then he added, "Where did you get this?"

Marcus broke out his South, "He's asking you a question, boy."

I said nothing.

"Well," Lucifer patronized, "we can find out," and he folded the paper. In one movement he dropped the note onto his desk and scooped up my phone. A second later came the sound telling me I had a new text message.

Lucifer flipped up the cover and displayed the message, "How's it going, handsome?" He positioned the screen so I could read it.

Jesus Christ, I thought.

"Whose number is this?" he asked like he had every right to know.

I was starting to feel uneasy about the whole inquisition but also kind of pissed. If they brought me in for the pipe, what was with all the questions about shit that had nothing to do with smoking.

Finally I said, "What gives you the right to go through my phone," I looked from Lucifer to Marcus, who had been mostly playing the silent enforcer so far, and added, "or to even do this search?"

Mr. Marcus took a step forward motioning in my direction like a traffic cop, "You need to close your mouth before you get yourself in more trouble than you already are," he spoke menacingly but that southern drawl made him seem like a cartoon character.

Lucifer was playing with my phone and frowning. My suspicion about the truth of the whole scene began to turn to violation. The way he clumsily mauled at the keypad made me feel like I needed to take a shower. His obsession with my phone was the sum total of the room's activity for a droning minute. Suddenly he broke his concentration and turned to Marcus.

"Parents coming?" he inquired.

"I think Mom." Marcus answered.

"Okay," Lucifer snapped like a drill sergeant, "Lets move it to the conference room."

He opened the office door and stepped into the hallway. I followed, but Marcus lagged. Someone in the opposite direction from the conference room called Lucifer's name, and he started toward the sound.

It wasn't a plan. It was simply the only thing to do. I sprinted the other way toward an exit.

I could hear their pounding footsteps following. People were yelling, but all I wanted was freedom.

It was maybe five seconds, and I was outside, running.

Running to get far away.

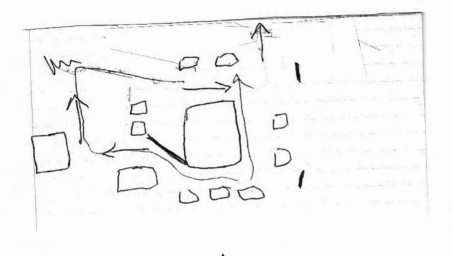

A

Fridays were always busier than other weekdays. The only other collectively busier time would have to be an actual time of day, and that would be any day about five minutes before we closed. I suppose it's a testament to procrastination as a national fault—this habit the general populace seems to exhibit of waiting until the last minute on the last day to send something through the mail.

I'd only been at the job a few weeks. It was a pseudo-post office type business established for the convenience of those who would rather fork out extra money for postage privileges than weather the USPS' certain ordeal. I liked it for the most part. I had laid back bosses who didn't mind my tattoos or frequent hangovers, and I could spend the periods without customers or packaging in any manner I liked. That was pretty sweet. It was my understanding that most businesses frowned upon employees using company time for personal endeavors. Since my most recent previous employment had been with the US Army, where there is virtually no "personal" anything, this job was like a perpetual hippie fest.

It was a regular thing for me to text or IM my friends, check my email, compose new blogs or make plans on the phone for evening festivities. That's how cool my job was. The owners were down with anything as long as there was no work to be done.

I got the call at around 4 pm. It was the store phone, so I was totally not expecting it to be a friend. Aside from the fact that my good friends know that unless they are in dire need of an immediate response I prefer texting, no one calls the store phone; they all have my cell.

"(Store name)," I answered mentally crafting professionalism.

The voice on the other end was breathless, rapid and familiar. The words instantly made my chest ache so I couldn't breathe.

Holy shit.

"Hey, have you talked to your mom?" He was never one for extraneous preliminaries.

"No. Why?" I asked, feeling a foreboding chill on both ends.

I listened to a rapid-fire synopsis of a harrowing afternoon, and as serious as my empathy was for what he had endured, all that kept cycling through my head was, "Omigod, Mom."

He was at a bowling alley. He had no coat, no money, no car, and it was freezing outside. He thought he could get a ride to my job. "Yeah, yeah, do it," I told him. I needed to know more if I was going to be able to instigate any serious damage control, and it would definitely take all of us to straighten this out.

I disconnected and thought of my mom again. My freshest memories of the inflexible authorities working for Uncle Sam crashed through my brain. I knew my mom would first and foremost believe in the triumph of good. For all her life-long hardships, she persisted in the belief that an honest explanation would always suffice, but just as fierce was her determination to protect those she loved. If she ever needed a semblance of my skill at calculated action, it was now.

I brought her up in my address book and selected "New Message." I kept it simple. "Deny everything," I wrote and prayed I was in time.

> **Smoke one more cigarette**
> **Now that we've met**
> **Because already our time is limited ...**
> **In a minute you'll be finished with it.**

C

I think they followed me for awhile. It felt like it anyway. I jumped some fences and flew through the residential backyards surrounding the school. When I finally had no more breath, I curled myself into a plastic tunnel that was part of a child's play set. I tried to gauge my safety while I waited for my breath to return. I knew all these streets. I had lived in this town the better part of my 17 years, but as I replayed my helter-skelter route, I could only determine that I wasn't far enough away.

I tentatively approached one end of the tunnel, emerging just enough to scan for movement. It looked like nothing but sounded like everything. Or was it all in my mind? The school, the office, the morning felt like a year ago . . . not even that . . . it was like it couldn't really have happened, so it was . . . no time ago. What made me sick, though, was the reality of what they thought was the truth, what they thought I knew and just wasn't telling. It was the horrible uncertainty of the gap between the two . . . I wanted to throw up.

I wasn't safe with my own thoughts. I crawled out and ran—to keep them from catching up. When I was forced to stop again, I climbed into a trashcan. I pulled the lid over me and blissfully the cold began to obscure all else. I had no watch. My phone was my regular attachment to time and that instrument was now some kind of warped evidence. I should have smashed it. I should have eaten the note. I should have run from the beginning. What I should have known is that it was only a matter of time.

Time. Again. I heard muffled street sounds but no voices. It was so cold. Who would be out here if they didn't have to be? I had to keep going, though. I had to tell them, but then we would have to tell "them," wouldn't we? Wouldn't that be the only way to straighten this out? They would believe us, wouldn't they? The cold kept me from thinking anymore. I needed to move.

Carefully I peered at the outside. No people in sight. It was like a neutron bomb had left all the non-living matter, and left a nuclear winter as well. Or maybe it was so silent and gray because that's how suddenly life had turned. *Just go.*

The next street gave me my bearings. I tried to stick just close enough directionally but far enough away to avoid detection. It felt like hours. I tried to figure out how long it had actually been. It became a game, a challenge in my head—like everything always did. Then I tried to estimate how far I had gone. Funny how people could drive a route over and over but still have no idea what the distance is. I was pretty good at stuff like that. I was probably right about the time and distance.

Unconsciously, I also had some semblance of an immediate plan. I had to get with them and, first, find out if they said anything to her and, second, what we should do. I didn't really know how schools dealt with teachers who they thought had broken rules, or, in this case, I guess they would think she had broken the law. Well, that would definitely be worse, but I'd had a possession charge 18 months earlier, and I wasn't at all sure how this new "paraphernalia" would translate. I did know that subsequent offenses inevitably brought harsher repercussions, but there was no going home on either score. M.L. was an asshole. For sure, he would make as much of this as he could. He didn't like her anyway.

Yeah, I was going to the bowling alley to use the pay phone. When I cut through the last batch of trees and saw the building, it was like for certain I could catch the carrot in the next try. Finally, stepping inside, I couldn't remember if heat had ever felt so welcome.

It took a few minutes to replace the ice in my bones, but I knew there was no margin built into this day's ordeal. As I rubbed my circulation up to speed I surveyed the sparsely populated lanes. Apparently this was not the hot time to bowl. I imagined I was squinting to locate a few bats in an enormous cave. Fortunately, one of the bats found me. A kid in my grade came up behind me, speaking my name. I didn't know him well, but we'd had some classes together in the past. The weirdest thing of the moment was that he'd already heard a rendition of my story. I'm sure his discovering me in the flesh was like winning the lottery in the gossip game, and in high school, this wasn't the kind of story warranting any bullshit intro.

"Hey, what happened today, man?" He was up with the protocol.

He obviously knew SOMETHING, so I figured I'd let him talk first.

"Some bullshit." Normally, I was a master at manipulation, but I was still fighting the serious fucking cold that was everywhere inside me. Yeah. I was a little worried, too.

The guy was pretty much just dying to tell ME what it was I had done, so it kinda worked itself out.

"I heard Lucifer was tryin' to search you, so you punched him and ran out." His eyes reflected his hope in this as the truth.

This guy was the silent type from what I knew, not one to be the first to get the scoop on shit of this caliber, but I also knew I was the kind of person he wished he could be like. In a second I calculated two ways in which he could benefit my current situation.

"Fuck that," I said, "I didn't touch him." I made sure number one was clear. "Yeah, he tried to search me, and I'm pretty sure that shit's illegal so I just dipped."

His eyes widened. He frowned. He juggled the two for a minute. "Did you walk here?" he finally asked incredulously. I could see he was creating a mental image of the distance.

"More like ran." I smiled as I said it but more because I got the sense of how a sarcastic hermit might relish his own personality after an eternity of seclusion. It felt liberating, but I had to stay with the plan. "So, school's out?" I asked him.

He looked at his watch. "Yeah, man, it's like 4:20."

I didn't have any more time. I just shifted into get-it-done. "Do you have a car?" I looked straight at him, but I'm pretty sure he knew whatever it was, it was serious.

"Yeah, man." He was nodding his head in corroboration.

"Could you give me a ride?" I started looking in the direction of the pay phones.

"How far is it?" He lifted his arm to see his watch.

"Like 5 minutes, "I answered, "Seriously, it's like one turn south off the boulevard."

He hesitated. "South, like, is it . . . ?"

I cut him off. "Straight up, dude, it's like 5 minutes from here. Can you drop me off?"

"Okay," he glanced over his shoulder, "you mean, like, now?" He scanned the lanes in back of me like he was searching for other people to alert to the plan.

"Yeah, thanks, man." I was in a hurry again. "Let me just make a phone call first."

Him being one of those quiet types, I couldn't tell if he was totally down and just patient or not-too-sure and subject to change without notice. I motioned with my hand what I intended to mean both, "Stay right there" and I'll be right back," as I kind of sprinted toward the phones.

It was pretty amazing that I had some change on me as I usually had so much other shit in my pockets that coins generally got thrown somewhere in my car. Then there was the fact that I no longer had a job, so having any money of any kind was hit or miss.

I had to call 411 to get the work number. Without my cell phone, I might as well have had no numbers at all. Besides that, I wouldn't have been sure which phone was safe to call. It was just better this way.

He answered the phone. That deep, even tone was incredibly relieving but simultaneously spurred urgency in me. I tried to just hit the crucial points, interjecting early that I had a ride waiting. I don't know if it was his age or his nature, but he always seemed quick to get the chase. I think there was a faint, "holy shit," at one point, but then he was all business.

"Okay, man," his voice rose, "I'll see you when you get here."

My ride got me there in less than ten. On the way I gave him the highlights of my trek from school to the alleys. It seemed only fitting payment for the ride; at the same time it solidified the tale in my mind. I knew I'd be telling it several times over.

This is pretty much what I told him:

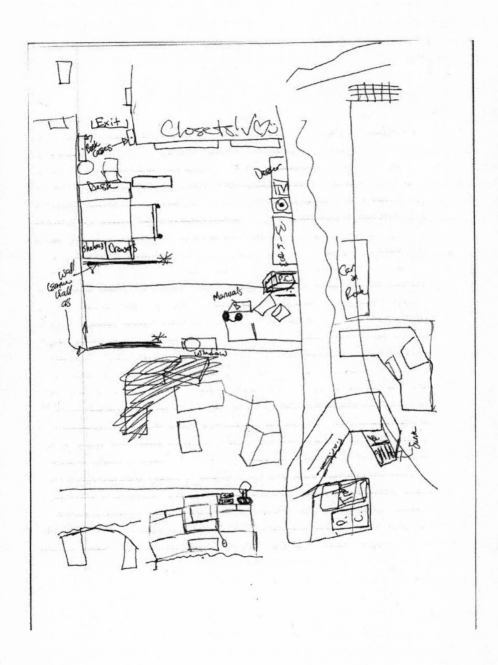

When I walked into the store, Aidan immediately crossed the room to meet me. He hugged me hard. I was so glad not to be alone in it finally. After a long second he stepped back. He gestured in a manner I always associated with his Sicilian ancestors, as he breathed, "Oh, man, what the fuck?"

W

It wasn't like I didn't know what he was talking about. Obviously he had heard something, and since it wasn't from me, I figured there was a lot more to the story. I'm fairly certain that if ever I was in shock, a functioning kind (if there is such a thing), it was at this moment. It was 3:30 p.m. School wouldn't be out for another 18 minutes, but school was over for me for now—for some nebulous amount of time over which I had no control.

I walked around my kitchen island trying to think but unable to slow the mental onslaught which flashed a textual collage on my brain:

> Deny everything.
> Did you write this?
> . . . administrative leave . . .
> . . . suspension with pay . . .
> Is this your handwriting?
> Morning, baby,
> Deny everything.
> Is there something you want to tell me?
> . . . not allowed on school grounds . . .
> Have you seen this before?
> Is this your phone number?
> Deny everything.

I wanted to call him, to talk to him, but it was too much for the phone. He was also at work. And where was his informant? How did he know?

It's lost in some protective mental device, what I did to occupy myself until the phone rang after 5:00, maybe after 5:30. He said, "There's someone at my work I'd like you to pick up if you don't mind."

It was barely half a mile from our house to his work. He was standing outside. No coat. I felt completely responsible for all that had been so incredibly misconstrued, but, not then and never after, for a second did I think of the truth as anything but pure. As we waited for my son to get off work, I heard the other part of what apparently clinched the accusation for the administration. They took a note from him in my handwriting.

There were text messages in his phone from my number. There were other things causing their suspicions; I knew what they were.

Aidan joined us at a minute after 6:00, and we drove home in silence. As concerned as I was for the unfortunate, bizarre turn of events, I thought (on that day) that resolution would be swift. Once I could tell my side, I thought they would apologize, and that would be the end.

I couldn't even have imagined how wrong I was.

A

Shit. I knew it. I knew it was just a matter of time. Goddamnit, I should have said "No" all the times she said, "Yes." It just became like a habit, and there were so many people here lots of the times. I guess I kind of stopped thinking that she could get in trouble. In the back of my mind, I think I have just always believed whatever she does has been perfect. If she's okay with something that goes against the general grain, I always side with her. I always want to have faith in her instincts; of course, if it benefits me, probably subconsciously, I definitely want to trust her. It's just that . . . , well, basically, I'd do anything for her.

I **know** she's done everything for me. Even what I couldn't understand at the time, when I felt destroyed and betrayed, there was always that truth in my heart. At this age, for sure, I question more, we loudly discuss more, but at the end I trust what she tells me. If she says it's gonna be okay, I believe her even if it scares me.

Probably the Army pushed me closer to this rebellion. God knows I was so tired of the stringent adherence to rules with little discernable rationale. Uncle Sam seems to relish that phrase, "because I said so." I'm fairly positive my mother never said that to me. I'm pretty certain I know her that well. She wouldn't want it said to her. That's how I know.

I was so glad to be out, out of a claustrophobic madness, out of a country where they hated us, out from under the peon status perpetuated by ignorant, undirected children desperate for power. I was so glad to be home, so excited to surprise her, so eager to see my friends and return to normal.

It didn't seem odd at all when I met him. I know people all over this area, and every party is an opportunity to meet more people. When he showed up at that party that day, all I was thinking is how we hit it off. I don't even think she was his teacher then. I think she just knew him through one of her other students who was his friend, and we didn't really talk about it. I know she was so glad I was home, and there were just a shit ton of people over all the time back then. Hell, if I went to her school, I probably would have had a lot more of her students at our house.

Fuck. Now what? How do I fix this for her? What can I do without having the power to turn back time? They don't really know anything about what's true, but I'm sure those bastards have already condemned her. I know that one asshole hates her. Fucking shit. It's the Army all over again. Do I have the energy to get out from under all over again—the energy for BOTH of us?

hold me closer
i just want to die like this
be in love with me for one more night
then you can go.

W

Okay, don't panic. It's all going to get straightened out. All they have to do is ask him, and he'll say they're crazy. It's simply that they don't know what's going on. They have jumped to their own conclusions, but when they hear the explanation all this will be over.

Yeah, that note kind of threw me. How did he get that? True, I didn't look at it this morning, I didn't think I had to. There is no way Aidan gave me that note this morning. Is there? No. Impossible. He would have told me, asked me. No. Not even. He wouldn't have considered it. Plus, that was a while ago. We're not even using that notebook anymore. How the hell did Caine get that? WHEN did he get it? What happened to the other note?

Shit, I can't be mad about the text. I'm sure it's happened before. The whole situation has gotten so familiar we don't even question it anymore. I'm pretty sure when Caine got the message he didn't think twice. Even though Aidan thought it was funny, it probably didn't even occur to Caine that it WAS from Aidan. I mean, my god, I use terms of endearment with my students more than I use their names.

So we're going home to figure out what to do. Of course, I'm more than a little freaked out, mostly because the administration immediately concluded I was doing something wrong. I know I didn't defend myself very well. I definitely shouldn't have said I didn't write the note, but I was so shocked to see it, and I knew how bad it looked. Then there was the text message . . . but even if I had used "baby" to address him, so what? Like I said, I use those terms constantly, in addressing male AND female students.

They're just trying to find something. Ever since Caine made one of his ISR goals to marry me and another teacher they've tried to . . . I don't actually have any idea what their objective is. Here's a kid with some issues already—very bright but obviously not stimulated enough by school to restrain him from "acting out." Yes, and how does the system handle stress, drug use and truancy? My observation is that it's with confinement, detention and restriction. How can it be that the failure of these punishments goes unnoticed? I mean, come on, what in the world is logical about suspension as a consequence for multiple absences? Sounds a bit more like a reward to me.

Often I wonder where some of these educators got their training. (I'm sure wherever you work, you, also, have wondered how people you work with ever got hired.) Let's just take Caine's ISR goal statement I mentioned a minute ago as an example. Here's the way it works when a student is assigned a day of In-School Restriction: Before students are awarded the privilege of doing the "real" work (that which they are missing by virtue of not being in class) they have to complete a form which requires them to elaborate on five goals they intend to implement in order to rectify the miscreant behavior responsible for landing them in ISR in the first place.

When they showed me the form Caine had filled out (my god, that was like within the first month of school, I think) it took me all of two seconds to see what he had been thinking when he wrote it. The form is on two pages: three questions (with plenty of room for a paragraph of recalcitrance for each question) on one page and two on the other. For heaven's sake, his first four responses were completely undecipherable. Oh, he'd filled up the page all right, but his writing was totally illegible. Then turn to the response to the goal concerning marrying me and the other teacher. His penmanship is so perfect it's excruciating. Now, does it take a psychiatrist or a rocket scientist to deduce that he **wanted** that answer to be read? If anyone (other than me) did determine that his clarity of writing was indicative of an objective, wouldn't that have been prudent? Doesn't it seem like someone should have at least asked him about such an obvious discrepancy? Wouldn't it have been in the best interest of the student for the administrators to try and attempt an understanding of such an apparent departure? Sure, there could be several reasons, but what do you think? The first thought entering my head was his effort to see if anyone really ever even read the things. Or maybe it was just his method of proclaiming what little respect he had for the school's system of determent. Whatever his rationale, my initial impetus would have been to let **him** tell me why **and** listen to what he was saying, but none of the administrators appeared interested in what seemed so logical to me.

As I recall when Caine was questioned about this goal of a relationship he proposed, he eventually got around to saying that he and I were friends. Apparently, Lucifer jumped right on that one, stating in no uncertain terms that I was his **teacher** and we were definitely not friends.

Caine says his response was, "No, we are. Go ask her." After a fraction of reflection he added, "If she says we're not friends, I'll pay for my own tuition to private school."

I can't remember exactly what Caine's punishment was for wanting to marry a couple of his teachers, but I vividly recall M. confronting **me** with the issue. He swooshed into the English workroom and started questioning me from a position way to invasive of my personal space. There were a couple other people in the workroom at the time, which I thought was kind of anti-protocol, but M.L. generally operated in his own 1940s Germanic fashion when he was on a mission.

"Willow," (I want to say, "he spat out my name," but, phonetically, it's difficult to spit a "w" or an "l." Let's just agree that he came as close was possible.) His eyes were nearly dangling from their sockets. "Caine Blaise is in my office right now, and he insists that you and he are friends." M.L. shook his head to indicate the general incredulity of his statement before he continued, "I told him—you are his **teacher** and not his **friend**, but he insists that, if I ask you, you are going to tell me that you two **are** friends."

I stumbled over my response. First of all I couldn't believe I was the only one who realized that Caine had been so blatantly testing the system and/or asserting his rebellion relative to this whole ridiculous thing, and second, . . . well, . . . the truth was . . . I **did** think we were friends. I felt I was friends with lots of students.

"Ahhhh . . . ," I tried quickly to figure an acceptable way to phrase the truth, "Actually, I . . . I **do** think we are friends." There. I couldn't lie.

Lucifer jumped on it immediately. "No, Willow, you are **not** friends with students." He paused for a second or two (I suppose formulating terminology which I could understand), "you may be **friendly** with students, but you are **not** friends with them."

Okay, I was at a bit of a loss there. All I could think was that the connotation of "friendly" conveyed a considerably more dubious suggestion than did the condition of being "friends," My silence was apparently interpreted as evidence of some serious wrongdoing based upon M.L's rapid additional explanation.

"You don't seem to understand." He sighed in exasperation. "This kid just told me that if **you** said you **weren't** friends, he would pay for his own private school education."

I had no other answer to offer. If the situation hadn't been so tense I might have pointed out Caine's creative expression in support of his conviction, but I knew Lucifer better than that. I had learned early in my teaching career the woeful absence in the actual classroom of implementation of cutting edge educational research. In other words, recognizing a student's linguistic, mathematical, artistic or physical ability outside of an accepted realm was virtually nonexistent. For sure, my adherence and abhorrence for that lack of recognition had brought me administrative grief in the past.

"I don't know what to say, M." I stammered at last, "'Friends,' 'friendly,'" I don't really get the difference." It didn't seem the time to express my views on the suggestive tone of one term over the other.

He was rigid all over. "Listen," he slowed his speech as if I hadn't understood all along due to a language or mental barrier, "you need to tell that kid, right now, in no uncertain terms, that you are **not** his friend."

Open-mouthed silence—one second. Cocked head—another second. Questioning expression—last second.

I knew in those three seconds that my only choice was to lie. If it had been any other of the four administrators in charge of English during my seven years at the school, I'm certain I could have pressed my position, but I'd had serious clashes in ideology with this guy the whole of the previous year. Now that I was department chair, I was doing back flips trying to shield the rest of English from his invasive power plays.

"Okay, M.," I finally sighed, "I'll tell him, 'we can be friendly, but we can't be friends.'" I know how I said it. I said it like I felt it: like it was the most ridiculous semantic garbage I'd ever heard.

It was only then he appeared to take notice of the captivated others in the room. Shifting his weasel frame nervously, he concluded with, "Make sure he understands." Then he flew out of the room as if some pressing engagement had suddenly occurred to him.

I was left thinking about all the students who would never be fooled by this linguistic rendition of our relationship, of the fact that every year the school made a tremendous effort to discover which "adults in the building" students felt they could trust (not "friends," apparently, just trustworthy adults)*, of how far the administration had moved from the intended purpose of the school, and, at that, why all I gleaned from getting my Masters in Educational Administration and Supervision was that I never wanted to be an administrator.

* I was on the committee responsible for this discovery effort. It was called "Student Support" or School Challenges," I can't remember now; we had so many committees. The second year of its existence I co-chaired the thing. Basically what we did was create a brief form (on a half sheet of paper) that looked something like this:

Name _____ **Grade**   9   10   11   12   (Circle one)
Homeroom # _____
Please write the names of at least two adults in the building (teachers, counselors, administrators, or other staff) who you feel know you and who you can trust.
1. _____
2. _____

That was it. We printed each grade's survey on a different color paper to make it easier to separate them when it came time to amass the results, because that's what we did. (I shouldn't say "we." The awesome technology assistants, who weren't/still aren't paid nearly enough, typed the monstrous load into a spreadsheet.) Each department chair got a copy of the final spreadsheet, categorized by teacher, and copied and distributed the list to his/her department members.

Now, think about it for a minute. What **is** the point of this? Let's say we really hope for/want all students in the building to feel "connected" to a couple of adults. How would a high school student feel connected to any of his/her authority figures? Think back to when you were a teenager. I don't pretend to speak for every perspective, nor do I consider myself a certifiable expert on the teenage mind, but I might know a little bit more about it than a non-high school teacher. My answer is, number one, an adult has to have the respect of the student, and respect comes in two varieties: the fearsome and the affable. Many students respect school staff because they are afraid not to—they have been trained in that fashion. The respect that garners trust, I'd say, is of the affable type. Students will talk to you if they believe you genuinely care about what they are saying. If they feel you listen to them, not just concerning the interpretation of a poem or a current event but about whatever it is they **need** to talk about. They respect an adult who cares what their home life is like, what their job is, what their dreams are. Wouldn't this be the kind of person **anyone** would consider trusting?

It hardly seems worthwhile if all we anticipated of a student-adult "connection" was the kind of standard interaction representative of the job! Imagine yourself, as a sixteen year old, feeling bonded over an understanding of the Pythagorean Theorem or a creative analogy of Woodrow Wilson's administration or the requirements for college applications. I'd be more likely to bond with the cafeteria staff who gave me extra french fries. A real bond occurs through specific accolades for understanding or through an analogy relative to the life of a sixteen-year-old or to the background of the **actual** college applicant. Forging the kind of connections I describe is part of what was once called (in **my** teacher preparation program) "the hidden curriculum" in educational jargon. It is part of what is only implied in the job description, part of a kind of on-the-job-training, part of why some people can't do the job.

Whether you agree with the previous exposition or not, its premise is rooted in my experience and a major contributing factor to my current outcast status. That being written, I give you the reproduction below, which has had these alterations: I numbered and underlined those points relevant to my particular situation for ease of reference. I numbered with a "G" and underlined those admonishments relegated to the category of "Oh, well," relevant to my particular situation. I deleted "member-type information" at the end of the brochure.

Adapted from[a] brochure prepared by Michael Simpson, NEA Office of the General Counsel. Copyright 2006, National Education Association.

1. <u>**Whenever possible, never be alone with a student.**</u>
   That's because a student's allegations made when there are no other witnesses hinge on credibility, and authorities often tend to favor the alleged victim in

these circumstances. So don't be alone with a student in a house or a car, and never give a student a ride home. To the extent possible, avoid being alone with a student in a classroom.

Risky situations include: one-on-one tutoring, counseling, after-school or recess detention, and make-up tests. If you can't avoid being alone with a student at school, keep the door open and stay in plain sight.

2. Always maintain a professional demeanor and distance.
That means: no flirting, teasing or joking about sex. Don't socialize with students or treat them as "pals" or "friends." Never give gifts, unless you give one to every student, and don't single out any one student for constant special attention or flattery.

3. Never send e-mails, text messages, or cards to students unrelated to schoolwork. Don't ask students about their social lives or comment on their personal appearance, and avoid discussing intimate details of your own private life. Don't hire students to baby sit or allow them to visit your home. Be the adult and maintain boundaries.

4. Avoid physical contact with students.
This is a particularly difficult area. Younger children often seek and need physical comfort from their teachers who, sadly, may be the only source of compassion and love that some students have. In the early elementary grades, an occasional hug is probably OK. But as a general rule, it's best to avoid most forms of physical contact, especially kissing, hair stroking, tickling, and frontal hugging. And use common sense: a "high five" to acknowledge a job well done is fine; a slap on the bottom is not.

5. Male teachers have to be especially careful when it comes to physical contact of any sort. While a female teacher's touch may be perceived as comforting, a male teacher's may be viewed as sexually suggestive. And male employees are far more likely to be accused of inappropriate contact with students than female employees. According to one expert, accusations involving female teachers and male students make up less than 5 percent of the cases.

6. Avoid using physical force when you enforce discipline.
When students are misbehaving or out of control, avoid touching or grabbing them to get their attention. Instead, use verbal commands and other disciplinary methods.

There may be a rare occasion when you will have to use physical force in self-defense or to prevent injury to others. If that happens, use the minimum force necessary to prevent harm and immediately call for help. Also, if this is a persistent problem, you may want to ask your district for special training.

7. Never allow a student to obsess over you.

While a crush can be flattering, it also can be fatal, so always nip it in the bud. An unfulfilled fantasy can result in a student acting out to gain attention or retaliating for being ignored. If a student expresses a love interest, respond with an unambiguous "no." Don't equivocate and certainly don't encourage the student by acting pleased by the attention. It's also advisable to share this information with another adult and your Association representative. In some circumstances, it may be appropriate to tell your supervisor and ask that the student be transferred.

8. Be particularly wary of "troubled" students.

This is a tough one. Some students come to school with a host of emotional needs and chronic problems, and they may confide in their classroom teacher and ask for support and guidance. Particularly for a student with emotional problems, a teacher's efforts to help unfortunately can be misconstrued as something more and may lead to an infatuation or dependence. Plus, you don't have the skills or training needed to assist.

While you can and should express concern and compassion, don't take on the role of confidant or counselor. Instead, refer the student to the school counselor, a trained professional who has both the expertise to assess what services the student may need and the experience to know how to arrange for the delivery of those services to the student.

9. Be especially vigilant if you hold certain teaching positions.

Anecdotal evidence suggests that employees who perform certain jobs are at increased risk of false allegations. These include athletic coaches and performing arts teachers—drama, band, chorus, and debate, as well as publications advisers. This trend may be the product of the intense nature of such activities, which may weaken teacher/student boundaries, coupled with a substantial amount of after-school, weekend and off-campus contact.

If the unthinkable should happen . . .

1G. <u>Don't talk</u> to school administrators or law enforcement officers. Even innocent statements can be misconstrued and misused . . . .

2G. <u>Don't sign</u> anything. It goes without saying that this will be an enormously stressful time, and you should not make any decision about signing a statement or other document without first discussing it with your representative.

3G. <u>Don't talk</u> to the media, unless and until you and your representative decide that it is in your best interest to do so.

4G. <u>Don't resign</u> from your job. No matter how bad things look, resigning will not help, and it may be interpreted as an admission of guilt. You should not consider this option until you have consulted with your representative.

. . . Sounds like a mantra: "Don't talk, don't sign, don't talk, don't resign." For heaven's sake, we are talking about teachers! These are people who perform a **very** difficult job, for a disproportionate salary, and, **in most cases,** because they **want** to, **care** to **TEACH**.

I will return to this later. You probably want to get on with the story.

C

Here she comes. Is she gonna be pissed or what? Shit, it's cold. I wish I had my coat . . . , hell, my phone, my wallet . . . all the stuff they took. Man, this is not good.

Aidan was awesome. The first thing he said when I got there was, "Are you okay?" I can just imagine my dad if I had gone home after this. He'd be like, "What the hell do you think you're doing? So now I'm gonna have the police over here? Whad you have on you this time?"

My mom, though? She would look all worried and say something like, "Omigod, baby, what happened? Where is your coat? It's freezing outside." Then she would try to get me to eat something.

Well, I can't go home. That's for sure.

I know something happened to her. Lucifer wouldn't let those texts go . . . Why didn't I delete them? The one fucking day . . .

Ok, I'm getting in the car. Aidan will be off work in ten minutes or so, I think. Shit, this is all my fault.

She looks as freaked out as I feel.

I'm so glad the car is warm.

"Ohmigod," she says, "are you okay?"

I want to get warm. I want to be safe. I want it all to be different.

She hugs me tightly. They say two outta three's not bad.

Love is the worst epidemic—over time and space and culture and creature . . . It changes everything forever—even though you think you are the same . . . all of a sudden nothing is as it was . . . and that is permanent.

A

Shit. Fuck. Goddamnit. I can't believe it. No, of course, I believe it. I knew we weren't being careful enough. I fucking knew it.

Okay, don't flip. Everything is straight, right?

People come to our house a lot. I have a lot of friends, and my mom is cool. Shit, I just got back from a fucking war. Wait, I don't think they call it a war anymore. What is it now? A conflict? An incident? A fucking ploy by our moronic president to disguise the fact that he's trying to secure oil reserves? Whatever. Jesus, I'm just glad to be out of that hell hole.

Finally, it's 6:00. I'm outta here. Damn, mom is freaked as hell. What did they say to her? More importantly, what did she say to them? I can't imagine she really said anything. Like that would be a huge conversation, and I'm sure those asshole administrators wouldn't even listen anyway. They already think they know everything, especially that Lucifer character. What a jackass—like he didn't give her enough shit last year. I guess it's worse now that she's the head of the department. His little plan to bring his friend from his last school on for the position failed, and he's just one of those guys with short-man-complex.

What the fuck? So, I'm like 5'10." I don't have to go around trying to screw other people just so I can feel good about myself. Prick. My mom is such a great person. All my friends love her. It only makes sense all her students love her, too. Why should Caine be any different? Okay, so he knows me? But I know a ton of people all over the place. It's not so weird that I would meet him.

I just don't want any drama, and I don't want anything bad to happen to my mom because of this.

I just don't want anything bad to happen to my mom.

For The Attorney

HIGH SCHOOL

Noise violation - C was here (not drinking) A hadn't seen a lot of people - they just started showing up. C went to Mom's b'day because he showed up at Aiden's job. No coat - said he had run away from school. A - called me, asked me to pick him up. In a rush - went to my brothers' house. Afterward I told C he had to go home - took him to a location near his house and dropped him off.

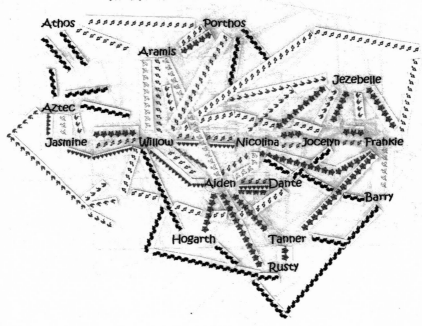

The Muskateers

Blood ～～～～

Close ♪♪♪♪♪

Special friends ⚘⚘⚘⚘⚘

Old ties ★★★★★

Love ♥♥♥♥

Tension ϟϟϟϟϟ

Acquaintances ～～～～～

THE REGULARS

The Genesis

The Regulars were all Aidan.

When he was discharged from the Army it was August. I was back at school for the teacher workdays prior to the students' first day. I thought he was coming home to me sometime during the first weeks of September, but he surprised me.

One of the main office secretaries came to the English workroom and told me there was something in the main office for me. I recall being just the tiniest bit aggravated—it was my first year as head of the department, and I had so much to figure out. If I had thought there was any possibility someone had sent me flowers (It had happened in the past but was personally unfathomable at the time.) I would have rushed, but it wasn't standard procedure for one of the secretaries to seek out the recipient of a delivery—I hate to say it, but her special effort immediately made me think that whatever it was, well, it was in their way.

I arrived at the entrance to the main office pretty much right away (more to get it over with than anything else). The office is a huge area with the two walls facing outward toward general student/visitor traffic being completely glass. Upon approach I was already scanning the floor space for some over-sized, offensive, we-keep-tripping-over-it package. I couldn't see it. No flowers either.

"Yeah, what?" I'm looking from one of the two secretaries to the other. They are both all smiles, giggling even.

"What?" I ask again. Even though I want to conclude this "adventure," I like the secretaries, and their obvious good humor makes me smile.

Here comes the athletic secretary now. (I mean she is the secretary for the athletic director.) Okay, her office is miles from where we are, and, like the others, she is grinning from ear to ear.

"Did you get your surprise?" she asks me.

"Not yet," I say wryly. All this clandestine mirth, I feel sure, will be anti-climatic.

The secretary who sought me in the first place is seated in her usual spot. She gestures over her shoulder. "It's in there." she tells me.

At the back of the room there is nothing "there," but a small closet. The door to this closet has never been closed, to my knowledge, during my entire years at the school. I always found that particular "open-door-policy" strange considering that all the copies of all the keys to open all the doors in the whole building were kept in that closet. I imagine there must have been a light, but I had never seen it on. Always there had just been a dark, gaping hole cut in the back wall.

"In there?" I asked the gleeful speaker. I was kind of curious now. The attendance secretary darted out of her adjoining office.

She looked around animatedly before focusing on me. "Oh, you don't know yet?"

"What? What?" I demand.

The original messenger is all frigidity in her chair. "Just go in there!" She points exaggeratedly. "It's in there!"

I tentatively advance in the direction of the closet remarking, "You all are scaring me . . ."

I'm almost at the entrance to the Netherworld. With every step I take, these four women are sharing a barely-containable, hilarious secret.

I'm on the verge of exclaiming, "I'm sorry, but this is too weird," when he steps out of the recesses into the light. He is my son. He is home. He is a second away.

When I scream, the impatient kindling sets the room on fire. They were all in on it. They were all privy to a most special kind of surprise. Of course, it was Aidan's idea to tell me it would be two more weeks . . . then arrange to overwhelm me, but . . . the secretaries (four women who I always thought just considered me statistics in a file) for that particular selection of moments, were an integral part of a relief and ecstasy I will forever have imprinted on my heart.

I squeezed my first-born baby so hard I couldn't think. The tale the secretaries would pass around all day was inconsequential to me. I only wanted everything else to disappear, so he would stay next to me, touching me, being part of me forever, and it would never be any different again.

You know how you can't imagine what it's like to have no legs or to get a knife put through your eye or to watch your house and all your belongings consumed by fire . . . unless you've lived it?

Whatever most incredible change **you** cannot possibly imagine—that is how much I couldn't imagine how different everything would become.

So they all came because of Aidan. Now that I know them all separately it's kind of curious that none of the steadfast Regulars were serious friends in the beginning (with the exception of Nicolina and Jocelyn). What happened is that our house became the "place you could always go." Once Aidan was back from Iraq there were a million nights in a row devoted to the activities of the Regulars.

In the next section my attorneys are introduced. Shortly after our acquaintance, I was fairly explicitly told to live like a hermit—for my own protection it was best for me to **not** have any visitors at my house, **not** socialize anywhere in my county and **not** talk on the phone or send email. The thing is, I had always welcomed Aidan's friends to our home in the past. Did the fact that I had been accused of some unseemly act with a minor suddenly make me unfit to allow anyone under the age of 18 into my house?

When I reflect now on the heyday of the group we started to call "The Regulars," it brings to mind the first line from *A Tale of Two Cities*: "It was the best of times it was the worst of times." Most likely that early-twenties crowd thought little more about their new environment than a change in venue had ever bestowed. If any aspect of the change garnered consideration, I'd say, without a doubt, it was the unfamiliar, regular attendance of me, Willow, their friend's mom.

Over and over in the last year I have doubted myself. I don't today come up with a word which satisfactorily expresses my state of mind for the many months ensuing after the administrative-leave-pending-an-investigation day. I'm sure there is a large group out there (maybe you, yourself) that will accept whole-heartedly the actions of my school's administration—the handwriting on the note which Lucifer intimated he recognized, the text with an obvious term of endearment. Later, I'll admit to many ways in which I consistently and blatantly violated school policies. You readers who will **see** only that should not be reading this.

I'm going to write my justification at the end of this sentence, and this is it: every action I have ever taken, relative to my position as a teacher, toward any of the 900+ I have had over the years, has been motivated solely by the purest intention. I freely give to you the confession of my unorthodoxy. Let me be clear, right here and now; these are transgressions I had committed for so long that I gave not a fraction of mental debate to any of the actions. I taught at that school for over seven years; my pattern and its increasing intensity over time was never, never anything but fodder for lunchtime sarcasm and amusement. Long before M. Lucifer began his McCarthy campaign, I had provided the basis for plenty of controversy.

I had parent-teacher conferences as a result of:

a) . . . remarking to a male student, "Research has shown that homophobia can be an indicator of closet homosexual tendencies."

b) . . . awarding a grade of "F" to a student who met the "four-page-paper" requirement by creating three inch margins on both sides of his essay.

c) . . . teaching Freudian criticism to my eleventh graders which necessitates the verbalization (aloud!) of the words, "penis" and "vagina."

I had teacher-administrator conferences as a result of:

a) . . . touching and/or using terms of endearment with students **and** other teachers.

b) . . . using a level of sarcasm which could be interpreted as demeaning to students **and** other teachers.

c) . . . exhibiting a general style interpreted as "anti-authority."

Now, before I abandon this stream, let me also enumerate that which has continually driven me deeper into my own destruction, it seems, but . . . you decide . . . at some point:

a) I compare each student to him or herself instead of to the representative "smartest" or to some standardized production out of Princeton, NJ.

b) I approach all these "children" (by definition) as if they are developing humans in need of collecting additional experience and **not** a completely different species requiring the opinions of others because they are incapable of having and/or expressing any meaning on their own.

c) I do touch them, males and females. I call them "honey" and "sweetheart" and "babe," males and females.

And I think they want to be with me (not **just** me, not **only** me, there are many other teachers with whom students connect and relate), because, although they have learned to behave at the hands of the system, they inherently want to be respected, need to learn to compare themselves to themselves, and some . . . some have never heard terms of endearment applied to them.

So, I'm guilty of expecting them to like me, to enjoy the variety I worked hard to include in my lessons, to tell other students in other classes how lucky they felt to have me as their teacher, and to never object to any of my methods. I didn't plan on this anticipation of mine. In the beginning I was consumed with giving my students a better understanding in a better, more exciting way. I really believed there was a style for every single one of them that would work. (I still believe that. The problem is the TIME required to develop higher thinking skills for the myriad of individual starting points.) It seems all that matters today, in virtually every public school system across the country is a particular pass rate on a standardized test.

I am so far off topic it's almost embarrassing to claim the teaching of English as my profession; one at which I believe I excel. If I can root out the relativity of this tangent, I'd say it is to explain one of the reasons I think the whole "Regulars" phase developed and why it lasted as long as it did. I know I started this whole section with, "The Regulars were all Aidan," but I think I needed them at the time they "arrived." I missed my students to a degree I would never have imagined before I was in all ways separated from them.

Part of the document spelling out my new status prohibited me from setting foot on the school's property. I vaguely remember skimming enough of the two brief paragraphs to ascertain that it was simply the binding reiteration of what I'd already been told, but it was that one commonplace phrase or directive, component, order, hateful-representation-of-how-impersonal-a-process-it-was which paralyzed me for hours after:

> " . . . you are restricted from _____ High School and you may not participate
> in any school division activities."

Unless you, reader, are or have been a teacher, it may be difficult to understand how devastating this statement was. Actually, you could even **be** a teacher and not feel how intense the trauma was, but, I swear, if you are any type of instructor who entered the field honestly and with purpose, you know what quickly happened to you. You morphed unconsciously, but hardcore, into an integral part of a living organism. You became the mitochondria of the cell which was/is your school. It's not like working for a CEO or a nebulous conglomeration of stockholders. If you are a real teacher you work for the students. Their parents may contribute the tax dollars or their hard-earned income, but you don't teach to please or placate or prove to them. You do it because you believe in your soul that giving knowledge and understanding to the future is of immeasurable value. If you aren't a teacher, my dear reader, at least you may be familiar with the sporadic surfacing of controversy over taxing the childless or retired grandparents in order to support education. I cringe with this pen stroke to recall one of my very first education courses in which I attempted to make a case of exemption for those without children. My professor responded immediately, perfunctorily and dismissively, "An educated populace is **everyone's** responsibility." End of discussion.

[EVERYTHING NEEDS TO MATTER FROM NOW ON.]
(I don't know why I wrote that)

I'm seriously making my way back to the reason for this whole section on the Regulars. The only effort at explaining my attachment to a group of 20-something-year-olds I am making is how the comfort they provided filled the void created by the absence of my students. Remember, this assessment is in hindsight, because as sure as practically 100% of the English speaking population will ascribe the color green to the entity called grass, I knew absolutely nothing approaching rationality at the time this whole ordeal began . . . and for many months afterward. But all that doom, gloom and death wish expression is in another part of this book. This is supposed to introduce the Regulars.

So, here you go. (If you have read this far you know I cannot present any dementia of mine simply.) Well, those spatially intelligent will appreciate my diagram representing the relationships between the Regulars. The designation, "Regulars" came about because of the frequency with which these people spent, let's say, often five out of seven nights a week at our house. I will spare you an anecdote from my teenage years which supports the fact that I had never had tolerance for a "party" with no directed action.

First, the Metaphor

Nothing is anything without a theme. The circus evolved as a mixture of drama and salvia. In short order I started making T-shirts for everyone and toward the end of the first phase of Regulars (the second phase is in Book Two), Aidan had devised a three-question verbal exam which the prospective Regular had to pass. Passing the exam was at Aidan's discretion. When you read Book Two you will get the chance to find out whether or not you could have been a Regular.

Second, the Original Carneys and their Functions

Willow	Mistress of Ceremonies
Aidan	Sword Swallower
Nicolina	Trapeze Artist
Jocelyn	Lion Tamer
Barry	One-Man-Band
Dante	Magician
Frankie	Magician's Assistant
Jasmine	Bareback Rider
Aztec	Clown

Then there were the Transient Carneys

Jezebelle	Contortionist
Tanner	Announcer
Rusty	Knife Thrower
Hogarth	Snake Charmer
The Muskateers	Escape Artists

The diagram which introduced this section is an attempt to explain for the visual/spatial learners what the relationships were between all these people. In referring back to it, keep in mind that the lines are fluid, and the whole illustration is about as dynamic as any situation can get. Now here's what they say.

Interviews with the Players

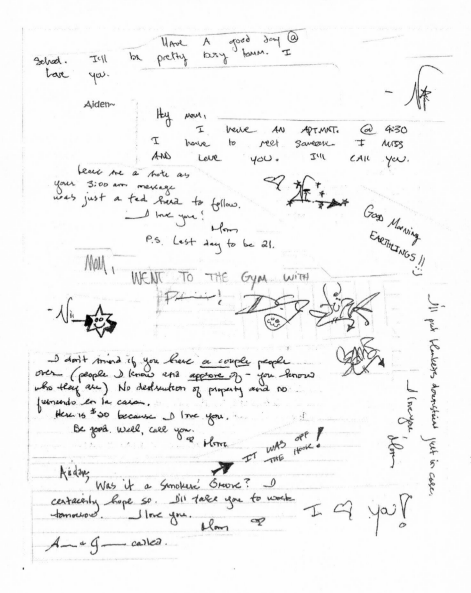

Nicolina ~

Of course, Jocelyn has been one of my best friends since high school, and she lived right there, practically next door. It was fun, but what I liked more than anything was that I could always be myself over there; there was no hassle. I mean, there were lots of times when a ton of people came over. Basically, if people were in town, Aidan would tell them to come over.

Well, I should just say right now that Willow was pretty damn chill from the first day I met her. Not that there weren't any rules but everyone understood them. Probably the number one rules was: No person steps foot in the house unless Willow says it's okay. So, when I said people would come over (there were **too** many on some occasions, if you ask me), I mean that was mostly before Willow got in trouble at school. Let's see Aidan came back from Iraq in like the end of the summer, but then he went to live with someone else for a while. I guess he moved back in with Willow around November sometime; that's when I started going there enough to be considered one of the hardcore Regulars.

Why did I spend so much time there? For one, Aidan and I connected incredibly. We had a lot of obvious shit in common: tolerance (in a variety of categories), disregard for any "normal" expectation, appreciation for pain, a deep understanding of struggle . . . god, we could talk for hours. We could talk like . . . like, there was pretty much no one else I could talk to the way I could talk to him. I'd definitely say he was my best guy friend at that time. I know most of the other Regulars thought Aidan and I were going to hook up. Maybe the two of us were the only ones who knew why that wasn't happening. Well, and Willow.

Like I already said, I thought Willow was fucking awesome about accepting all Aidan's friends, because, in the beginning, we were all Aidan's friends. Like somebody would be on their phone telling whoever it was where they were, and they would always say, "I'm at Aidan's," even if he wasn't there at the time but Willow was. There came the day, though (maybe toward the end of the winter), when that got reversed. It's kind of funny now that I'm remembering it all. One day it was just, "I'm at Willow's." Whenever that was, Willow and I were really close by then.

I guess there were times, probably early on, when it crossed my mind that she was my mom's age, could be my mom, but that's so irrelevant now. It's not that I'm not close with my own mom, but I could talk about anything with Willow. Maybe she didn't judge me or try to give me advice all the time because she **wasn't** my mom, but I don't really think that was why. I think she's just like that. Look, I know I can fluctuate between being social and being anti-social pretty quickly and in ways some of my friends would give me shit about, but however I was never bothered Willow. You just don't find too many people like that. I don't care how old they are.

Plus, she was like me about all the drama: it was just pointless and immature. No, she never really commented out loud to anyone (unless she was making a joke out of it, and most of them couldn't recognize the sarcasm anyway), but the better friends we became, the more I could see how much we were the same. Well, she was/is Aidan's mom.

I loved the games. I'm sure we started with MADLIBS®. I don't remember if it was me or Willow who first introduced them as what became one of our common activities, but they were fun as shit! Sometimes I would just do them by myself, especially when the others were talking about stupid crap or I just didn't feel like thinking. I've always had this habit, not on purpose, of just tuning out parts of what people are saying. Willow says that's part of my style of intelligence, like I only consciously tune into what a person is saying if my mind recognizes it as important. Maybe that's what attracted me to MADLIBS®: each person only has to come up with one word, but every word is important.

The more MADLIBS® we did, the more creative we got. At first I'm sure that was me. Hah! When I was the one with the pen, if I didn't like the word someone gave, I'd just say, "No," and some of the babies would cry, but Willow was totally down with it. Maybe because she was a teacher, I don't know, but she would always push the game. I mean, when we started it was okay to just give whatever part of speech it was, then there was no repeating, then nouns had to have an adjective with them . . . It got kind of crazy trying to write everything in those small spaces (and I write **BIG**).

I guess I could just tell stories I remember about being at Willow and Aidan's with the other Regulars, but most of what I remember probably wouldn't be the best stories because, as I said, a lot of it was drama, and that's all bullshit to me. What I can say is that the crap Willow was going through was drama **and** bullshit, but I told her one thing many times. I wish she had been my teacher in high school.

Jocelyn~

Ohmigod, in the beginning? It was awesome. First of all it was so close. Even if I had a whole bottle of wine to myself, I could just walk home. Or I could just sleep there and know there'd be no hassle, no planning or effort or worrying about how the hung over crybabies were gonna get anywhere. It was fun, too. Usually we'd talk for a while—people would catch up if they hadn't seen each other or there would be that standard "rehashing" of a recent night's antics.

Mostly, well, Aidan was fucking entertaining as shit. Man, when he was "on," it was seriously contagious. I mean, Nicolina is my best friend; I love her to death, although she does have her moods. (Okay, so do I, but when I don't feel like socializing I stay home. If Nicolina decides to go out she is **however** she is **wherever** she is. All I'm saying is, some nights she'd just sit on the couch and weave bracelets or lie on the floor with her eyes closed—not talking to anyone. I don't care, she's been how she is since I first met her, and I love her anyway. My point here was only to say that Aidan was almost 95% of the time what they call, "the life of the party."

Another thing was I liked how we usually **did** something over there. We did a lot of MADLIBS® then we got Catch Phrase. I think most of that was Willow. Yeah, I guess in the beginning I wasn't sure about hanging out so much when Aidan's mom was always there, but, after a while, it just seemed normal. I mean I always knew she was his mom, but, at some point, I just didn't think about it anymore.

Jasmine ~

Shit, Willow? She was/is seriously my best friend. We met when we both worked at the restaurant, and since then we have been through a ton together. I remember when I first started dating Aztec, I'd go to work hoping, hoping she was working, too, so I could talk to her. It was so hard breaking up with my last boyfriend. (He worked at the restaurant with us; he and Willow were friends, too, which made it even harder.) Once I was definitely with Aztec, we hung out at Willow's all the time.

It was so fun. Sometimes there were a bunch of people, mostly when Aidan was home. Well, he had been home from the war since, since, I know it was around when school started because I remember how he surprised Willow at school. Oh my god, she was so happy! Look, she's had it tough with her kids. Their dad is always making it hard for her, and it so weird because she is like the best mom. She thinks about her kids all the time, and shit, works three jobs so she can see them and do stuff for them. Oh, yeah, and she has to pay child support 'caz they live with him (except Aidan, of course). Now that's fucked up, and you want to know why? Because he is like a billionaire!

Maybe you're thinking I just take her side since she's my friend, but I've met all Willow's kids. They pretty much get "the life" living with their dad—if "the life" is never having to worry about clothes for school or lunch money or, say, ever going on a vacation. Okay, I guess that's what I always wanted. That and for my dad to be happy, not fight with my mom. But this isn't about all my shit; it's about how cool it was to be part of the Regulars.

I don't remember how It started, probably Aidan, he's so quick to pick up on the way things are. Ohmigod, you should see him freestyle. Somebody will just put on a beat and he goes. I could never do it. He makes comments about people in the room, that are funny—all the time, his rhyming and keeping to the beat . . . And it's all real, what he says! It all makes sense and it matters.

Anyway, he probably started calling us the Regulars. Let's see, it was me and Aztec, definitely Barry and Frankie were together then, Nicolina and Jocelyn. Caine used to come over in the beginning. Then I think he started bringing other people, and I think Aidan and Willow had some problems with it. I'm not sure. I am sure that when Jezebelle started showing up, practically living there . . . Shit, holy hell broke loose after that. It was after Jezebelle came that so much changed.

Over the summer, the Regulars were a lot different. There was still me, Aztec, Nicolina and Jocelyn, but Barry was gone 'caz he and Frankie broke up. Frankie was definitely gone, but that's a whole other story for Willow or Aidan to tell. All I would say about any of that is, "I saw that no good bitch-bastard comin' a mile away."

Okay, I'm running out of time, and I don't want to forget to say that although Aidan was/is a serious "life of the party" attraction, Willow was the stabilizing force. It's kind of strange—I never thought that much about it at the time, but she made the t-shirts, she brought out the games (damn, even before Scattergories, she had her own version where everyone just needed paper and something to write with. (Yes, it was during one of those games when I thought a beaver was a type of dog. Can we let it go now?)

Willow turned us all on to **doing stuff**. Yeah, we were drinking, but no one watched TV or played video games like at a lot of other "parties" I've been to. Willow always wanted there to be meaning about what we did, what we talked about. It seemed like she was always thinking of how we could be entertained using just our minds. Wait, I have a great example of what I mean.

One night Willow and I were chillin' in her room, talking, catching up on a bunch of shit, (Oh, I should say that at this time, Frankie was downstairs. I thought she was mad at me so I was kind of hiding out in Willow's room). About 1 am Willow went downstairs to talk to Frankie about something, and while she was gone I got a call from a number I didn't recognize. Normally, I would have ignored it but Aztec was known to borrow other people's phones to call me when we weren't out together. I just assumed it was him.

The voice I heard almost paralyzed me, every inch. Without telling a **huge** story of my own, let me just tell you that this girl calling (who used to be such a good friend that we got our first place away from home together. There was a time—ask willow 'caz she know the bitch too, from the restaurant—when this girl and I were both inseparable, if we weren't with our boyfriends, but they both worked at the restaurant, both part of the elite bartenders and both regularly down with us all chillin' together.)

Yeah, quickly, we got an apartment together. I gave her cash for my part of the bills. Three months into the lease I woke up one morning to find that she had moved out because we were being evicted for being two months behind on rent! She left a note. The general idea was:

> I'm sorry, Jasmine. I spent the rent on recreation. I didn't want you to know the situation so I hid the multiple eviction notices we received. Anyway, the police are coming to throw us out at 7:30 in the morning. I'd hide some stuff if I were you.
>
> > I love you,
> > Charlotte

I won't go into what happened that day and the nightmare that followed. I only needed to set up why the phone call I got at Willow's that night made me go ballistic.

This call is the first I'd received from her in the almost nine months since that day. So willow comes back from talking to Frankie to find me hysterical on the phone. No, more than hysterical—it was like the Tasmanian devil had joined the Navy and become a crack head. I'm cursing at top volume, occasionally pausing to catch fragments of her incredible reason for calling—"Jasmine, can't we just forget it and move on?"

Now Willow is with me. Blah, blah blah . . . , and I finally hang up on the bitch. Willow commiserates for a while then tells me that Frankie (remember, downstairs?) is not at all mad at me and wishes I would come say, "Hello." My friend encourages me. I think she knows it would benefit me to regale someone else with Charlotte's atrocities to help get it out of my system. So I trek downstairs.

Whew! Finally, here's what I want you to know about . . . my friend, Willow, why she's my best friend. While I was reiterating my tirade for Frankie, Willow stayed upstairs writing this:

1:00 a.m. Charlotte calls Jasmine to apologize for her lame-ass, fucking, unconscionable actions. OMG, C's on the verge of waterworks, she's sooo broken up over it all. (Now **that** noise is the background for a different sound bite.) Then she magically orders the cessation of her tears to make way for our new beginning and says, "So, how is your life Jasmine?"

What would Charlotte most like to hear Jasmine say?

A.) Probably pretty much like yours only I'm sure not as good. I like the people I work with, but most of there are trying to get employed at your place. I'm taking classes, but you are further along than I am. Gosh, it was so big of you to call considering I'm so beneath you.

OR

B.) Hey, I'm terrific, thanks for asking. Yeah, you did fuck me over but my boyfriend says I should put you out of my memory. He says Paris is a good spot to replace memories, so he's taking me there for three weeks in October. No, I'm sill deciding what kind of work suits me. Stephen tells me I should take a couple years, and, you know, see what really interests me. I mean, he makes plenty of money to support us. Well, he doing modeling for Calvin Klein right now, but his family got lucky in the stock market years ago. He has his eye on the cutest 28 room bungalow up in Westchester.

OR

C.) What the fuck are you calling me for? What is it your sorry about? What happened? Why don't' you tell me since I've been pretty much asking myself that question since January.

C: I fucked up.

J: Tell me about it.

C: I'm saying I'm sorry.

J: And I'm saying, what exactly are you sorry for?

C: That I fucked up.

J: Jesus Christ! That answers nothing. Do you not know? Can you really not tell me what you did to me?

C: Let's just put all that behind us.

J: Put a fucking chainsaw behind you.

C: Jasmine, aren't you over it? I am. I subscribed to the Barbie Fan Club, and it's changed my whole life. My hair is still dyed blonde and I had to get implants so my bust measurement would equal my hips, but I'm seeing this really cool guy named Ken. So far he's redecorated my apartment in the most awesome jungle motif, and we can wear each other's clothes. He's mad ubersexual. We haven't had sex yet, but it's only been six months, and he does have a medical condition called Soreanus—one of those inflammations that only flare up on the weekends or at night, or around one of those portable johns in the park, but anyway, what's going on in your life? Anything even as remotely close to as fantastic as mine?

J: Burn in hell BITCH!

C: I did burn some toast the other day. Ken is so resourceful though. He scraped off the black part and showed me how to make an exfoliant by mixing it with non—fat mayonnaise.

J: And fuck Ken too!

C: I don't' know . . . I told you I haven't even

J: Oh for Christ sake, dumb ass. (Click)

C: Jasmine? Jasmine? Wait, do you want an awesome recipe? Ken calls them fudge packers! Jasmine? Are you there?

When Willow read it to me, I just died laughing. She's the best.

Porthos~

The first time I was ever at Aidan's I went with Aramis. I guess he'd been there before 'caz he took us straight to the back of the house and started climbing up this fence to get on the deck. Aramis is kinda crazy, but he's been my best friend for a long time so I never question what he does much.

I could hear the music from the street, so I doubt anyone inside could hear us climbing up. When we got on the deck the door was open so we just strolled in. There were a bunch of people in the kitchen listening to Aidan freestyle. When we came in, Aidan just shouted something like, "Whoa, man, they're coming in from all over the place!"

I don't think at that time The Regulars had been thought up. Back then it was just a really good party with an interesting, stimulating, and unique group of friends. I definitely have to say it was always a good time over there, though, and I looked forward to hanging out with that bunch.

Yeah, Willow, uh, Ms. Kincaid, she had been my teacher, but I had always felt like she cared about me. I didn't think it was too much of a stretch for us to be friends.

From Willow ~

I know, there are more Regulars who'd like to speak, but it seems better to introduce some of them when they inadvertently get mixed-up in my shit.

LEGAL REPRESENTATION

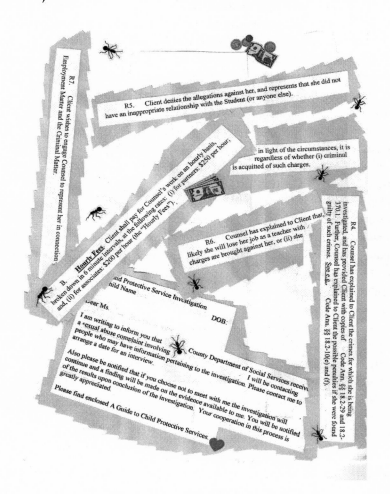

R5.   Client denies the allegations against her, and represents that she did not have an inappropriate relationship with the Student (or anyone else).

R7.   Client wishes to engage Counsel to represent her in connection Employment Matter and the Criminal Matter.

in light of the circumstances, it is regardless of whether (i) criminal is acquitted of such charges.

R4.   Counsel has explained to Client the crimes for which she is being investigated, and has provided Client with copies of   Code Ann. §§ 18.2-29 and 18.2-370.1. Further, Counsel has explained to Client the possible penalties if she were found guilty of such crimes. See e.g.   Code Ann. §§ 18.2-10(e) and (f).

B.   Hourly Fees: Client shall pay for Counsel's work on an hourly basis, broken down in 6 minute intervals, at the following rates: (i) for partners: $250 per hour; and, (ii) for associates: $200 per hour (the "Hourly Fees").

R6.   Counsel has explained to Client that, likely she will lose her job as a teacher with charges are brought against her, or (ii) she

and Protective Service Investigation
child Name

DOB:

Dear Ms.

I am writing to inform you that a "sexual abuse complaint involving people who may have information pertaining to the investigation. Please contact me to arrange a date for an interview.

Also please be notified that if you choose not to meet with me the investigation will continue and a finding will be made on the evidence available to me. You will be notified of the results upon conclusion of the investigation. Your cooperation in this process is greatly appreciated.

Please find enclosed A Guide to Child Protective Services.

County Department of Social Services receiv   I will be contacting

Ray & Diana

F or the last several years I had considered forgoing payment of the monthly dues to the Educational Association, the closest thing we had to a union, but my best teacher friend always said, "Don't do it!" He provided some clandestine rationale involving teachers getting in trouble, needing representation, how the association would pay for it . . . . Of course, most years I had thought, "Well, that will never happen to me," but he was so adamant that I continued my membership out of respect for him. It actually wasn't prohibitively expensive. I just didn't feel fifty bucks of fruition every month.

I called their local office on Monday morning and had an appointment for the next day. The representative I spoke with over the phone had explained that the standard procedure was for me to meet with one of the attorneys specializing in the legal ramifications of teacher suspension. At the time I was fairly incredulous that there was a "standard procedure" and lawyers who only represented teachers who had been suspended. It seems a lifetime ago when I was that naïve. She informed me there were two attorneys currently associated with their office but only one of them was available the next day. What did I know? I still thought it was going to get straightened out in a matter of days. I told her, "Fine, fine," to everything.

On Tuesday I sat at a table for twelve with two other people: the association representative I had spoken with and the attorney, Ray O'Hanlon, who was to become one of my few links to sanity over the coming months. I told them a bare sketch of my story. Certainly I had been prepared to tell everything, but there was, for real, a standard procedure which necessitated only enough information so the association could justify applying for the attorney's services. What I remember exclusively about that particular meeting is that when I related why I had a close relationship with Caine, the woman from the previous day's phone conversation said, "That's what I thought." Hearing her comment was the first brush of sunlight in my mental painting entitled "The Morass." I really don't remember how long I spent with her that day: I just know I felt like someone actually understood.

I met with Ray shortly thereafter. It could have been the next day. His office is fairly close to my house which turned out to be a good thing since I was to visit him quite frequently over the ensuing seasons. I think I spent a good two hours with him that first time—part of it was paperwork, but most of our time was spent with me detailing the events leading up to the moment Fangboner thrust that paper in my face.

A couple weeks after that initial meeting Ray explained to me that we needed another attorney on my case—a criminal attorney. Keep in mind that from the day I first met with Ray I had been advised to not talk about anything relative to my situation, on the phone, to anyone. For the first two months of this ordeal, I spoke to no one except my son, select Regulars and Ray. After "The Family Storm" I did speak to my mother and brother sporadically but everything had to be in person, so (aside from my overwhelming depression, which prohibited the desire to communicate) I was slowly developing a reclusive habit which further restricted my interaction with others.

I had no idea what I was doing / supposed to do, so I said, "Okay, another attorney . . . ." I was introduced to Diana de Fiamma the next time I met with Ray. Bulldog or pit bull: that was my first impression. I'm pretty sure I cried more during the meeting at which I was introduced to her than I did at any other meeting I had with the various authority-type-individuals with whom I ultimately came into contact. Let's see, it was at least the middle of January when I first encountered Diana.

I know it was before the police raided my house, before my mom and brother accusingly accosted me over it all, but not before I was subpoenaed for fingerprints and a handwriting sample. I guess the timeline doesn't matter much anymore, but you need to know that **at the time** . . . that factor, "time," was **everything**. It was **everything** for many reasons, all reasons to which I imagine each reader can relate at some point, on some level.

Time was crucial then (forever after, really) because it affected:

> My job/income
> My child/children
> My social/work relationships
> My habits/routine/schedule

As I continue relating the story it should be obvious how much influence all these outside forces exerted on every aspect of my life, but maybe only in the case of a natural, non-human-caused disaster can anyone else realize this type of devastation. Out of respect for chronology, I am doing my best to tell it in the order in which it happened.

So, before Diana, there was handwriting and fingerprinting, but, before that came the Monday "After the Weekend."

AFTER THE WEEKEND

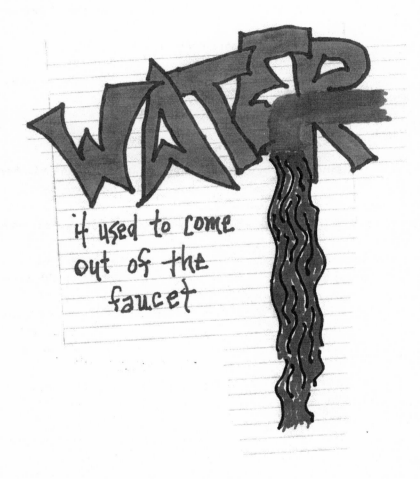

WATER
if used to come
out of the
faucet

W

The Monday after, I'm not sure what time it was except I know I assumed Aidan had gone to work because it was after 9:00. The phone rang. It was Jocelyn telling me that two cops were walking up to my door.

They knocked, even though I have a doorbell.*

I felt two ways as I walked toward the front of the house. The first was scared because I'd never had any real interaction with police outside of a few tickets over the years, and I couldn't imagine why they were coming to my house. The second feeling I had was indignation. I could only imagine that their arrival was relative to the most recent, unbelievable happening, and they had a lot of nerve thinking I would immediately accept them as part of it. After all, it was my school administration that put me on leave. I vaguely remembered hearing the word "investigation" the previous Friday but never anything about the police.

Here is the unedited transcript which I wrote that day:

Monday, December, 12:45 pm

Doorbell—two men identified as police (Adolph showed his badge) asked if I was me. Said they were looking for Caine "Is he here?"

I said, "No."

"Can we have a look around?"

I said "No."

"Ma'am, Caine is a fugitive. If he's here, you are in a lot of trouble for harboring a fugitive."

I said, "He's not here."

(One of them said to the other—"We need to get this over with—these guys have other calls to make"

"Then why can't we come in?"

I said, "I need to talk to an attorney first, I just got off the phone with someone who told me not to talk to anyone until I meet with an attorney."

Adolph said, "You don't have to talk to us, just let us walk through your house."

I said, "I don't think you can just come in my house if I don't want you to."

Adolph said, "The fact that you don't want us to come in makes you look suspicious."

I said, "Well, you just wait and let me call her and ask if I should let you in."

Adolph said, "We have a warrant for him, he is a fugitive. Is he here?"

I said "No, I told you."

"Then you have nothing to worry about. Just let us come in and walk around."

I said, "Are you going to destroy my house?"

"No. We are only going to look for any place big enough for Caine to hide in—like closets and under beds."

Reluctantly, I let them in.

They told me to show them around.

We walked through the first floor. They told me to turn the lights on. We went downstairs. The other guy told me to turn the lights on.

I said, "They are on."

He looked out the back door. He pointed to a closed door across the room. "What's in there?"

I said, "The laundry room."

He opened the door, "Where's the light?"

I said, "It's burned out."

He asked Adolph for a flashlight. Adolph said he didn't have one. Then he asked me if I had a flashlight.

I looked upstairs then went down and told him I didn't know where it was. (He also tried to get one from a 3rd officer outside—this guy didn't have one, but came inside at that point)

There are two doors inside the laundry room. He asked me what the closest door was.

I said, "A bathroom."

He asked, "Is there a light?"

I said, "Yes."

He opened the door, turned on the light, went in and pulled back the shower curtain. Then he opened the other door (my son's bedroom). I couldn't see past him, but I heard him. "What's your name?"

My son (who was in bed) said, "Aidan Kincaid."

The officer said, "Let me see your hands." I couldn't hear what else he said for about 20 seconds. Then I saw my son standing next to his bed. Both original officers were in his doorway, the other was writing down info from Aidan's ID.

I said, "That's my son."

The guy said, "I'm just writing down his info."

Adolph said to Aidan, "You want to come upstairs for a minute."

I said, "*That* is my son, he is sleeping."

Adolph said, "It's for our protection."

We all went upstairs.

We went to the top floor. Taylor stayed in the kitchen with Aidan. Upstairs I opened all the doors. They looked in all the rooms and under my bed. We went back downstairs. The other guy told Aidan he could go back to bed.

They walked to the front door.

Taylor said, "You don't have to say anything, but I'm going to make a blanket statement to you—if you know where Caine is and you aren't telling us, it's going to be worse than it already is—and you know what I'm talking about."

He wrote down his contact info and said, "I am the person investigating this case."

Then they left.
It was about 1:10 pm

*As you can see from the transcript they must have rung the doorbell, however, after they raided my house with a search warrant a couple months later, I became skittish whenever there was a knock on the door. It became common knowledge among all regular visitors that knocking could get you left on the doorstep or, at the very least, severely berated.

Nameless individuals, who have had more experience with the badge-carrying protectors of someone else's interests than I have, convinced me that knocking is their general MO. My available logic concludes that knocking is a guaranteed alert, whereas, maybe a doorbell is out of commission (or one could claim so). What follows from this rationale is that the police do not want a house's occupants to have any reason to delay opening the door. If this is the case then either they automatically assume some guilt on the part of the people who live in the house or they are just naturally very impatient individuals. I wonder how that segment of cop orientation goes. Maybe something like this:

Chief: Okay, you new people just remember—always knock on the doors. Never ring the doorbell. Any questions?

Recruit: Why shouldn't we ring the doorbell? Wouldn't that be more polite?

Veterans: (laughing) Rookie! Moron! Won't last long!

Chief: Settle down, folks. No such thing as a stupid question—except this one. Son, where did you get the idea that we are supposed to be polite?

Recruit: Well, I just thought, I mean, what if they're nice people who didn't do anything? I mean what if we make a mistake and are at the wrong . . .

Chief: (yelling) Are you insane, boy?! They've all done SOMETHING! They are all guilty! Even if it's not what we think, believe-you-me, they're all hiding something.

Recruit: (quietly) Gee, sorry, I didn't think . . . didn't know . . .

Chief: It's okay, son. Most of 'em have no idea they are all criminals. That's what makes our job so damn tough.

Veterans: (nodding) Amen, boss. Amen.

Anyway . . . as soon as they left I called the association office and asked the representative about the legitimacy of this police visit. She said, "By no means did you have to let them in. Absolutely not."

Like I said before, I'd never been in trouble, and apparently I don't watch enough TV because it seems I was the only person in the world who didn't know that I didn't have to let them in.

So Aidan and I discussed this most recent turn of events—how I shouldn't have let them in (all right, already), the fact that they didn't have a flashlight and, after bullying their way into the house, had the audacity to ask **me** for one, what the hell the third guy was doing outside **and**, most incredibly to me, did they not even know what Caine looks like? They needed to look at Aidan's ID to know he wasn't Caine? I told Aidan how it freaked me out when I heard them say, "What's your name?" because I thought he was at work . . . wait . . .

"How come you aren't at work?"

I listened to a whole new story. A few minutes later I went back to the laundry room.

"Hello."

In retrospect I see how I was still strong then. I was still myself.

A

Holy shit! Yeah, I guess if I had gone to work like I was supposed to it never would have happened. At the same time I thank the Army for the fact that it didn't really freak me out once I realized what was going on. I think mostly it was the voice. You hear that commanding tone; you've been programmed to follow the issued instructions. Plus, I've been "out there" enough to generally know the drill.

Cop: Put your hands on top of your head! Keep them where I can see them!
Cop: Let's see some ID.
Me: My wallet is over on the dresser. My military ID is right on top.

After they were satisfied with my identity, they let me put some clothes on, but they also wanted me to come upstairs with them. It wasn't until they stepped out of my room, and I began searching for some sweats that it actually formed as an idea in my head. They were looking for Caine. Why did mom even let them in? Did they have a search warrant? And where the hell was he?

C

Oh, yeah I'm going home. Sure, I can see that shit storm now. And it'll last all weekend.

For sure the school called. Hell, even without what was on me, they'd have to tell my parents that they'd "lost" me. It's kind of funny in a way. I mean what if one day a bunch of kids just ran out the door right in front of some administrators? Shit, they be freakin' out, trying to call for reinforcements on their radios. Look at how many followed me and for how long? Fuck, they'd be in some deep shit for losing a bunch of kids.

But I can't stay out here forever. I got no fucking coat, and it's fucking cold. I wish I at least had my coat. That mother-fucker, Lucifer, man, I hate that asshole. The way he talks to you, like my goddammed dad.

Yeah, my dad. I can hear it now. Same shit over and over. Sometimes I wonder what he'd do if he didn't have all the "bad" things I do to focus on. It's like he just waits for the next time I fuck up so he can yell and scream at me for hours on end. No, fuck that. I can't go home.

But my mom . . . she's worried I know. It has been almost two days. How long is it a person has to be gone before he's considered "missing"? I think it's 48 hours. She wouldn't call the police though. She knows me. She knows I left school 'cause there was trouble. She knows I haven't gone home 'cause there'll just be more trouble there. Yeah, my mom is awesome.

Still, the school had to call her, and someone had to get my car. If they gave her all my shit she knows I don't' have my coat. Fuck! I mean she knows I have a lot of friends. By now she's definitely called everywhere she thinks I might be . . .

Okay, shit, I'll just call her from the pay phone, just tell her I'm not frozen somewhere. *Just don't take long. Let me go and do it now.*

Veronique: Hello?

Me: Hey, Ver, is mom there?

V: Caine? Where are you?

Me: I'm okay, just get mom, okay?

Mom: Caine?

Me: Hey, mom.

Mom: Oh my god, are you okay, baby?

Me: I'm okay.

Mom: Where are you?

Me: At a phone booth.

Mom: No, where? Where is the phone booth?

Me: With some friends in . . .

Mom: Honey, come home.

Me: I will, mom.

Mom: When?

Me: Soon.

Mom: That doesn't tell me much . . .

Me: I gotta go, mom.

Mom: Well, I love you. Please come home.

Me: I love you, too.

If it was just her I would be going home to . . .

W

Monday was a holiday I think, or maybe I just couldn't get an appointment with the area chapter of our educational association until Tuesday. I didn't really anticipate needing a lawyer for much, but I hadn't gotten my Master's degree in educational administration for nothing. I learned it was always the first thing to do. Wow, when I think back and remember how many times I thought, "Certainly this will be resolved in a week, then, okay, it is Christmas break, they just haven't gotten around to it, but . . . , well, there are mid-term exams to get ready for, then give exams, grade exams . . . It wasn't until the police arrived at the end of January when I probably accepted that I was unable to predict when it would be over.

Maybe my experience being fingerprinted and giving a handwriting sample should have partially prepared me for the police raid on my house in late January, or maybe nothing can prepare a person for a home invasion perpetrated by those one assumes are in the business of protecting people's rights. Yes, Ray had told me there would likely be a search warrant issued so the police could legally enter my home, but, stupidly, I thought it would be more like an appointment and less like a rape. Come to think of it, maybe it was the fingerprinting and handwriting which led me to believe that the police would call first. (I feel like an idiot even typing that.) Here's what happened then . . .

FINGERPRINTING AND HANDWRITING

I received a letter from Ray shortly before Christmas telling me that the police had a warrant for my fingerprints and a handwriting sample. I wasn't surprised at the request to determine if my handwriting matched that on the note Caine had when he was hauled out of ISR, but the fingerprints . . . all teachers have to be fingerprinted before they can get hired as teachers. Not only had I been fingerprinted three times in the last seven years—having worked as a teacher in three different counties—but one of those counties was this very one which was now requesting it be done again. I wondered what had happened to all my other fingerprints, wondered if any agency actually even did anything with all those teacher fingerprints, wondered if fingerprints changed that much over time . . . but none of this ever occurred to me again once I experienced what "real" fingerprinting is.

Following are the transcribed notes I wrote right after I left the police station that day. The numbers at the top of each section refer to the number of note pages I used to write it all down. ("1" is the first page I wrote, "2" is the second . . . you get it.) I don't know why I thought it was important to retain that information. Probably it's because the only notepad I had in my possession at the time was a little 4x6 deal from my school; the original typed lists below all include a banner across the top advertising "my" school with the logo of "our" mascot. I suppose I just can't let the irony go. Any explanatory information I have added is in parentheses.

1

FBI—6 cards: individual prints both hands, individual fingertips both hands, full palm both hands, side palm both hands
LC (Local County)—6 Cards:
Individual prints both hands
-Flat
-Rolled SS (Secret Service)—3 Cards:
"Writes" palm both hands, index finger both hands
Handwriting

10 cards:

Name, address, DOB, other personal stats

Write the alphabet (in both capital and lowercase)

8 addresses (random but complete with name, street, city, state and zip code)

20 full names (first, middle and last)

2

Handwriting (cont):

20 sheets of lined paper: (Yes, I wrote it twenty times.)

Adolph dictated the "note" (the one Caine had when he was "busted" in ISR)

Comments:

Initial instructions for the HW (handwriting) cards

Adolph: "Just breeze through it." After about 5 he said, "I've seen your handwriting and it's neater than this. You need to take more time."

Me: "You told me to 'breeze through it.'"

Adolph: "Yes, and you follow directions well, but now try to take your time."

3

Pertaining to the dictated "note":

After about 14, Adolph: "I don't think I've seen this before, but as you're getting tired, your writing is getting smaller." (chuckles) "If we keep going we won't be able to read it."

Me: "So you want me to write bigger?"

Adolph: "Just write your normal handwriting."

Me: "I don't even know what my 'normal' handwriting looks like anymore."

4

Random conversation between Adolph and Ray while I was filling out the HW CARDS:

No order (in these bits of their conversation)

—Where is what in Ohio? (I don't remember "what.")

—The etymology of the term "cop"

—NY city (Ray's upbringing)

—NY state (Adolph is from there.)

—Adolph traveled a lot upstate last summer

—How people don't' write much due to computers

—Adolph's career history

5

Adolph advises Ray on his BIO (looked it up on "Nextel"?)

"Your full date of birth is on there"

Identity theft (They talked about this possibility.)

Adolph asked me often during the HW "phase" if I wanted to "take a break"

During the cards I asked if he had any food. Ray asked if I felt like I needed to eat. I said "Yes." Adolph suggested candy. I said, "I can't eat that."

Adolph thought there was a vending machine somewhere. It was discovered, and I bought some PB (peanut butter) crackers

6

While I was buying crackers, Ray (told me later) asked Adolph how long he though the investigation would take. Adolph deigned to give a time but said something to the effect of "as quickly as possible."

Murders in the (local) county (Ray and Adolph discussed them.)

Adolph, Ray and I are all 47 (years old . . . I believe Ray brought this to the room's attention.)

The whole thing lasted about three hours. As I type this, it has been roughly three weeks since I retrieved a lot of documentation from Ray's office. He had advised me early on that anything I had written down about the "investigation" should be left with him for safekeeping.* This is the first time I've actually read every word of the notes from that day in almost a year. Here are some of the thoughts I had at the time, organized by heading number, which come back to me now:

1A. Couldn't these various organizations (FBI, SS, LC) share this information? I'm talking 15 cards in all and of pretty much the same thing. Isn't this the age of technology? Or is it true what they say in the movies? That all the various divisions are super territorial and competitive? And so, what's up with that?

1B. The handwriting part was the worst. Can you see how much writing that was? On each of 10 different cards I had to write all my personal information, the alphabet twice, 8 complete addresses and 20 full names. Come on, now. Does a person who specializes in analyzing handwriting really need all that? Wouldn't 2 or 3 suffice? And if he/she DOES need 10 cards . . . sorry, but his/her tuition money went to a charlatan.

2A. I started to cry somewhere around the 13th time I had to listen to Adolph dictate and write, "I think we should . . . have sex . . . ." I cried for a couple reasons. One was because I was tired and hungry and angry and demoralized by this point. One was because my hand might as well have been engaged in some kind of torture designed for confession (maybe it was). But mostly I cried because they just didn't understand. They never asked me anything about why I might have written such a note, if I did or who I would have written it to. I was just a "bad guy" from Day One.

2B. I can't help it. I have to say, "Breeze through it . . . Take more time"? Make up your mind. What? Like it wasn't already obvious (after 3, 4, 10 cards) that the handwriting on the note matched mine?

2C. And " . . . you follow directions well . . ."? Don't patronize me, asshole.

3. Did you realize how many rules there are relative to providing the police with a handwriting sample?

4. OMG! I love Ray; he's been fabulous throughout this whole thing and stayed with me the whole time that day. I'm sure he was attempting to introduce a familiarity which might kindle Adolph's altruistic side (if he had one), but, Jesus, all that small talk was driving me insane! All I could think was, "WHO THE FUCK CARES?!"

5A. Blah, blah, blah . . .

5B. The majority thinks candy is food. It's so sad.

6A. Yeah, "as quickly as possible," my ass.

6B. That was the culmination of the small talk—that we were all the same age. I can't even contemplate (even today) all the twisted meanings possible relative to that summation.

* safekeeping—once again, it should have meant something to me. Like I should have known that Ray meant they would terrorize my house, stealing anything they interpreted as remotely related to my alleged crimes, but I still didn't get it. I had no idea how devastating an uninvited visit from the police could be—until that day.

THE INVASION

W

I drove Aidan to work and returned home around 11:00 am. Frankie and Barry were sleeping on the futon downstairs, but I didn't know it at the time. I'd only been back about ten minutes when there was a ferocious knocking on the front door. I rushed to see who it was because the intensity and severity of the knocking clearly spelled urgency.

Looking out the peep hole only informed me of the fact that the perpetrator of the interruption was a person unknown to me, and he was not alone. I was paralyzed by confusion but definitely headed to confront the situation.

I opened the door as I were saying, "oh, my gosh! Are you serious?"

The following is the transcript I wrote of that day:

1/27 11:30

Banging on the door, someone yelling, "Police! Search warrant!" I opened the door.

First Cop (FC) pushes me back into the corner. Says, "Stay where you are and don't move!"

Me: What is this about?
FC: It will be explained to you.
Me: Don't you have to show me something?
FC: It will be explained to you.

(After it seemed as if 50 cops flooded my house, Adolph appeared.)

DT: Just stay where you are, Willow. Somebody will talk to you in a minute.

About ten minutes later this other cop (OC) tells me to sit on the couch. Gives me the warrant. Tells me to read what they are looking for.

Me: Can I get my coffee?
OC: I don't think you need to be sipping on coffee right now.
Me: Hey, I'm not a criminal.

Barry comes up from downstairs in handcuffs. Maroon-Shirt Cop (MSC) calls Adolph downstairs. Barry and Frankie each go in the kitchen separately. I don't know how long they were in the kitchen, but eventually they were directed to sit on the living room couch next to me.

While Barry and Frankie were sitting on the couch with me, and their stuff was still downstairs, the MSC called Adolph to go downstairs. After Adolph came back upstairs, the MSC came back up and threw Frankie's purse onto the couch next to him. (Barry's socks and Frankie's bra were in the purse.)

MSC: Anything else downstairs?
B: My cell phone is down there. (MSC goes down and gets it.)

MSC went back downstairs three times to get more clothes for them.

There was one more thing asked for but I don't remember what it was. I know the third time Frankie asked for his scarf. After that he took a bra out of the purse.

F: Excuse me, boys, I need to put my bra on. (He walked to the powder room.)

(Barry and I exchanged glances, wondering if the cops could tell about Frankie's particular predilection.) Then Barry and Frankie got their shoes and coats on and went outside with the MSC.

MSC: (Outside) You were this close to getting a summons because you lied to me, but this is your lucky day.

About ten minutes later, Aidan came in. The Cop-in-Uniform (CIU) asked him to empty his pockets, checked his ID.

Me: Adolph, can I call my attorney?
Adolph: (Hesitates) I don't see why not?

He wouldn't give me my cell phone, just looked in my phone book and gave me Ray's number. Neither Ray nor Diana was available.

I asked them all repeatedly not to leave the doors open so the cat wouldn't get out. Older Guy (OG) in a suit came upstairs, asked if it was okay for the cat to go out, because she was out.

Me: NO! I told you guys!
OG: Sorry.
Me: Oh my god, what are you going to say if she runs in the street and gets hit by a car? Sorry?
OG: I can't get (him). Adolph, can she go out and get her cat?
Adolph: Yeah, okay.

I went out and got her. The MSC was outside trying to call her. When I came back in, I asked if could put her upstairs.

Adolph: Just put her in the bathroom by the front door.

I am reluctant because I usually only put her in there if she's bad, but I'm afraid to say anything. After about ten minutes the cat starts meowing. I take her out and hold her, but she keeps trying to get away.

Me: Adolph, could I please put my cat in the bathroom upstairs? The one down
        here is punishment to her.
Adolph: (Sigh) wait a minute. (Goes upstairs and returns after five minutes.) Okay.

Aidan arrived about 1 pm. He saw several neighbors looking at the house—police cars and CSI (Crime Scene Investigation?) vehicle parked in front of the house. For a second I didn't even recognize him. People just came in and out like they owned the place.

Me: Hey, baby. (I was so relieved to see him.) You didn't have to come home.
Aidan: (Sits next to me on the couch.) It's ok, mom, are you okay?
Me: I've been better. I just wanted you to know what was going on.
Aidan: Mom, it's okay. I didn't want you to be by yourself.
Me: Thank you, baby.

The CIU was standing near us but didn't speak. After half a minute Aidan stood up and spoke to him.

Aidan: Oh sorry, you want to see some ID?
CIU: Yeah, if you don't mind . . . uh, just empty your pockets.
Aidan: (complies) I don't have a driver's license. There a worker's ID and my
        military ID.
CIU: Okay, you're fine. (He continues to stand.)

Aidan and I talked about his leaving work. I was worried about that. After a few minutes I said to the CIU, "Don't you want to sit down?"

FCO: Sure. (Sits on the loveseat.)

Chatted about nothing for awhile then

Aidan: Is it okay if I smoke?
CIU: (Calls into the kitchen) is it okay if he smokes?
Adolph: I guess, if you don't mind.
CIU: (To Aidan) It's okay with me.

A minute later Adolph calls out—tells him to go outside. Aidan, the CIU and I went outside. Not much until about 2:00 pm when I got tired of sitting down and walked to the window. Then I could see Adolph and some other cops reading all MY shit in the kitchen. I just started feeling so violated and demoralized. I started to cry. Aidan came over and started hugging me, telling me it was okay. That lasted about five minutes.

A Swearing Cop comes through and said they were almost done. Then he added, "If it were me, after all this, it'd be Miller Time." He sat down and was rattling on, swearing with abandon. (I realize that he is the same as the FC who had a battering ram at the door, caused a scene outside, and shoved me in the corner.

About fifteen minutes later Adolph came in and said, "I'm sure you have other things to do. I know I do."

Then he handed me the inventory of what they were taking, and Aidan and I start reading it. When we see the first two items, (Adolph had put the 2nd part of the list on top of the "formal" list), Aidan and I both say, "Those are not ours." We point to them on the inventory sheet.

Adolph replies, "We didn't say they were, just have to put it on there." He won't look at us as he says this.

They all leave. Thank god!

The ordeal lasted until about 3 pm. I needed to pick up my daughter, Phoebe, at four, and Aidan or I (can't remember) called my mother and asked if she could do it. I hadn't eaten all day. Aidan made me a tuna salad sandwich. You know how everyone's mom makes some food that is so familiar and comforting that it just can't be duplicated—even with the exact recipe? (Spaghetti sauce and turkey dressing come to mind.) Well, my son makes the most completely tasty and satisfying tuna salad ever. We just call it tuna fish. Ever since he was about 16, I'd say, "Honey, would you make tuna fish, if you have the time?"

Unlike the human majority, neither of us has ever been much enamored of food except for its necessity for living. I doubt, under the circumstances, that I would have been able to eat anything else. Aidan was fabulous throughout the whole horrible experience. People cavalierly toss around the phrase "I don't know what I would do without you," but, as of that afternoon, sitting in my kitchen, overcome with the fallout of dread, I knew he would forever reign supreme when it came to that sentiment.

Willow's Aftermath

I ate a little of my sandwich, then I went upstairs.

Apparently the cops take a few more liberties if the homeowner is out of sight, because these are the notes I took on what I saw:

Jackson's room: Everything was pulled out of the closet and thrown in a heap in the middle of the floor.

Phoebe's room: Everything in the closet was still in the closet but all in a jumbled heap.

My room: In the top right dresser drawer, a sachet had been ripped open and potpourri was scattered all over the clothes. In my jewelry box a baggie with three baby teeth (from the tooth fairy) was ripped open—one tooth was left in the bag, one was on the dresser and one was in the jewelry box. Aidan's baby book was half out of the bookcase. When I tried to straighten it out, a picture of Aidan fell out. It was ripped almost in half.

Powder room: French maid toilet paper holder had her fingers broken off.

I was so depressed from seeing the third floor I couldn't bring myself to go to the basement level. I went back to the kitchen and sat down. Even though Adolph had given us the list of what they had taken, I hadn't gotten much past the audacious lie of the first two items. Now, as I turned my head apprehensively in various directions, I began to notice some of the specifics of what was missing.

There were bare spots on the refrigerator where pictures had been. It's funny that you could see something everyday for months, maybe even years, and at the same time **not** see it. I had to think hard to recall which pictures were gone.

1. An extended family vacation we had participated in over the summer. It was of my daughter, one of my nieces and two of my nephews. They four of them were wearing bathing suits and striking one of those popular "gangsta" poses.
2. Aidan and Jackson's very recent birthday. It was a close-up photo of the two of them and was symbolic in the sense that (being five years apart in age but born on the same day) it was the first year they had felt old enough to share a party with both groups of friends.
3. Family day weekend when Aidan was on leave from Army Basic. It was a picture of Aidan and two of his buddies acting ridiculous for the sake of the camera.

I imagine the common denominator of the three missing photographs was that they all contained males ranging in age from 13 to 21, and I suppose that is the full scope of possible ages for high school students. I can't pretend to know what was going on in the collective mind of the police, but it does seem to me they should have at least recognized Aidan since he had been sitting on the couch in the living room throughout this particular tyranny.

Some of the items on the schedule of inventory were as easy to recognize as it was painful to realize. Most of these generic effects were communicative in nature: my daily planner, the computer, two cell phones, at least two of Aidan's journals and his jump drive. Let me just show you the complete **AFFIDAVIT FOR SEARCH WARRANT**. I apologize in advance for all the blacked out sections, but at the time I'm writing this the case has not been closed, and that's pretty much all I need right now is for the police or the county to try and act as if I had somehow defamed **them**. When there appears information necessary for understanding the document but deemed too identifying, I've inserted what I hope is blatantly fictional.

AFFIDAVIT FOR SEARCH WARRANT

CASE NO.

The undersigned Applicant states under oath:

1. A search is requested in relation to an offense substantially described as follows:

   Criminal Solicitation   (Class 5 Felony)
   Indecent Liberties With A Child   (Class 6 Felony)

2. The place, person, or thing to be searched is described as follows:

   The interior and any attached storage areas of a townhouse residence identified as ▓▓▓▓▓▓ - the sixth townhouse unit from the left and third from the right when facing the front. The front of the unit is slightly recessed from the other units in the row and is described as a 2-story brown brick townhouse with finished basement. The front of the townhouse has burgundy shutters next to the windows, white trim around the main entrance door, and is clearly marked with house numbers ▓▓ next to the main entrance door. There is a tan clay pot beside the sidewalk leading to the entrance. There is a tree and some shrubs in front of the unit. The back of the unit has ground level double-glass sliding doors located under a first floor deck that leads to a downstairs den and bedroom. There is no fence in the back yard, and there are pine and other trees located there.

   (□ CONTINUED ON ATTACHED SHEET)

3. The things or persons to be searched for are described as follows:

   Any and all electronic devices including desktop and laptop computers and palm pilots, accessories to include all power supplies, monitors, keyboards and printers, all electronic storage media devices to include but not be limited to floppy disks, CD's, zip drives, and other external drives, and all electronic documents, all print film and digital cameras, including all developed and undeveloped print film and printed or non-printed digital camera electronic storage media, all pictures, photographs, e-mail, text messages, and handwritten or typed letters and notes indicative of possible illegal activities, all cellular telephones including camera phones, all audio-video and audio recording devices and recordings, all personal telephone directories and notes containing names and telephone number notes, all sexual enhancement instruments and devices relevant to this investigation, and any and all controlled substances and paraphernalia will also be confiscated.

   (□ CONTINUED ON ATTACHED SHEET)

   (OVER)

COPY

AFFIDAVIT FOR SEARCH WARRANT

APPLICANT:

NAME _____ Investigator

ADDRESS _____

Certified to Clerk of _____

County Circuit Court on

Delivered to Clerk of _____ County _____ Circuit Court on

/ _____ TITLE _____ SIGNATURE

_____ by the undersigned

Magistrate _____
TITLE   SIGNATURE

4. The material facts constituting probable cause that the search should be made are:

I received a complaint on Friday, December X, XXXX reporting that 47-year old Willow Kincaid has been seen in the company of a 17-year old juvenile herein known as "C.B." one on-one at work on more than one occasion. An administrator reportedly counseled Kincaid about not being alone with juveniles. Kincaid and C.B. reportedly call and text-message each other frequently and have each other listed in their cellular telephone directories. The administrator's concern was heightened during a meeting at work on December X, XXXX regarding a possible device used to smoke marijuana found on the juvenile when the juvenile was also found with a sexually specific note. The note bore handwriting closely resembling Kincaid's writing and stated that "I think we should see how many days in a row we can have sex…how many times each day…and how many different ways. See you tonight." A small heart was in place of a signature. Finally, C.B. had several business-card size Christmas party invitations in a wallet announcing that guests should bring "drugs, coke, drinks, lingerie (real sexy)" to Aidan Kincaid's (Willow's) on December X, XXXX from dusk until dawn."

I later determined that Aidan Kincaid is Willow Kincaid's 21-year old son.

Kincaid is an adult caretaker responsible for C.B.'s safety and well being.

5. The object, thing or person searched for constitutes evidence of the commission of such offense.

6. ☑ I have personal knowledge of the facts set forth in this affidavit OR

   ☐ I was advised of the facts set forth in this affidavit, in whole or in part, by an informer.
   This informer's credibility or the reliability of the information may be determined from
   the following facts:

(☐ CONTINUED ON
ATTACHED SHEET)

The statements above are true and accurate to the best of my knowledge and belief.

Investigator
TITLE OF APPLICANT (IF ANY)

Subscribed and sworn to before me this day.

DATE AND TIME

☐ CLERK   ☐ (x) MAGISTRATE   ☐ JUDGE

I had some questions pertaining to the **AFFIDAVIT FOR SEARCH WARRANT**, but none of the 15 adults present on the day of the search seemed interested in allowing me to move or speak or even have coffee, for god's sake. I sure as hell didn't expect they felt like answering my questions. Sigh. I guess that's why a person always needs a lawyer. When I finally could breathe steadily and my eyes were no longer swollen from crying, I read every word several billion times. It is possible that the questions I have stem simply from semantic interpretation, syntactical errors or standard legal requirements. Remember, I was, I still am an English teacher. Maybe I'm just too picky or suspicious or willing to find fault, and if that's the case, I guess I'm just like them.

Either way, there is the glaring difference in that no one ever asked me for an explanation after the very first day, the day I was put on academic leave, whereas I constantly desired answers for what felt like grand-scale misuse of power and exponentially unnecessary tactics. Let me not neglect to add what twisted inside me beyond all else relative to the "investigation": the increasing knowledge that a basic tenet of our country's justice system, "innocent until proven guilty" was, in reality, its exact opposite.

I had no one to talk to except Ray and Diana, and, although I did write down the questions I had (see below), I did not write down my attorneys responses. The parts of the document with which I took issue are followed by my rationale for confusion and any recollection of legal explanation.

In #2 and #3: "the things or persons to be searched . . ."—No persons are listed, so how were they able to search Barry and Frankie? I believe the explanation was something along the lines of "people in the place are assumed to be part of the place, or they are things found in the place." Am I the only one who then wonders why the word "people" is even included? Oh, certainly, it's to show the humanness of the system.

In #4: "material facts constituting probable cause . . ."—Pretty much it is that contradicting string "facts constituting probable" with which I have problems. In science I am of the mind that facts are relatively indisputable. If I am correct in my knowledge of the scientific method, it is the initial hypothesis which is the "probable" part. What becomes a generally agreed upon fact is the result of proving that determined to be probable. If my logic is sound, this appears to be another case of phraseology which is in fact the exact opposite of my understanding of truth. Well, you decide. My lawyers were too cryptic on the matter to be understood. Just for my own satisfaction I've distinguished that which I consider factual from that which might be probable and just had to provide a category for the ridiculous:

Factual—

> " . . . seen in the company of a 17-year old . . . known as 'C.B.' . . ."
> " . . . have each other listed in their cellular telephone directories."
> " . . . found with a sexually specific note."
> " . . . A small heart was in place of a signature." (Recognize that the note was not addressed to C.B.—not addressed to **anyone**.)
> " . . . Aidan Kincaid is Willow Kincaid's 21-year old son."
> "Kincaid is an adult caretaker responsible . . ." (See myriad restrictions on caretakers' implementation of responsibility in the NEA brochure reprinted in the section of this book entitled, "AT SCHOOL.")

Probable—

> " . . . one on-one at work on more than one occasion."
> " . . . An administrator reportedly counseled . . . ," (Who reported this?)
> " . . . reportedly call and text-message each other frequently . . ." (Who reported this and what is his/her evidence?)
> " . . . handwriting closely resembling Kincaid's writing . . ."
> " . . . responsible for C.B.'s safety and well being." (See myriad restrictions on caretakers' implementation of responsibility in the NEA brochure reprinted in the section of this book entitled, "AT SCHOOL.")

Ridiculous—

> " . . . Kincaid [should] not be . . . alone with juveniles."
> "The administrator's concern was heightened . . . regarding a possible device used to smoke marijuana found on the juvenile . . ."
> " . . . had several business-card size Christmas party invitations . . . guests should bring "drugs, [etc.] . . . to Aidan Kincaid's (Willow's) . . ." (I know nothing about this.)

In #6: "I have personal knowledge of the facts . . ."—How does "[Adolph] have personal knowledge . . ." as opposed to being " . . . advised of the facts . . . by an informer." I was particularly incensed by what was an obvious choice made by Adolph when he checked one of the boxes. To me, personal knowledge would be his own witnessing of what he is claiming. Isn't making a claim based on the reports of others considered hearsay? Isn't hearsay inadmissible as evidence under the law? Aside from that, it incensed me even more that the implication was he knew me, knew my son, knew Caine, and that notion falls squarely under the heading of RIDICULOUS.

Once again, I'll let you decide based on electronic transmissions which I supposed constitute the personal knowledge Adolph gained from two different interrogations. The first one is an instant message (IM) conversation between Caine (designated by "me") and a classmate of his. The classmate's name is blacked out for protection. At the end of the IM exchange are pieces of a brochure sent to me (Willow) from Child Protective Services.

me (7:29:39 PM): hey

me (7:29:52 PM): tell me everything that happened, now, please.

▉ (7:29:56 PM): ok

▉ (7:30:08 PM): he asked me if i ever partied in ▉ county

▉ (7:30:41 PM): i said know he asked me like are you sure? he asked the same question multiple times but like in different ways to see if i would change my story u know

▉ (7:30:51 PM): he asked if i had ever partied with anyone from there

▉ (7:30:52 PM): i said no

▉ (7:31:07 PM): he asked if i had ever been to a party where a teacher showed up

▉ (7:31:10 PM): i said no

▉ (7:31:20 PM): he asked if i had ever hung out with a teacher

▉ (7:31:21 PM): i said no

▉ (7:31:43 PM): he asked if i knew anyone that had and i said no but i told him about ▉ and how she like did a substitute

▉ (7:32:45 PM): he said i told him enough and that if he needed more he would be in touch

me (7:33:30 PM): ok

me (7:33:50 PM): did he say something about me

▉ (7:33:53 PM): that was pretty much it

me (7:33:55 PM): or ask anything about me

▉ (7:34:41 PM): no he said that some boy was at a party and an he said that something happened to him that the boy didnt think was bad but he did

me (7:35:45 PM): anything else

me (7:36:18 PM): did he say anything about that "something" that happened to that "boy"?

me (7:36:33 PM): or anything else

■ (7:36:38 PM): no

me (7:36:43 PM): ok

me (7:36:45 PM): thanks

The report concerning your family or a child in your care has been determined to be appropriate for an investigation response.

WHAT HAPPENS DURING AN INVESTIGATION?

During an investigation, the CPS worker will:

- talk face to face with the child, the parents, and the alleged abuser/neglector

- observe the child for injuries or signs of abuse or neglect

- observe the child's home

- interview or observe the child's siblings

- check for previous reports of abuse or neglect

- contact other persons who know about the child such as doctors, teachers, or relatives. You may assist in identifying these persons.

WHAT HAPPENS AFTER AN INVESTIGATION?

When the investigation is complete, the CPS worker will determine if the report is founded or unfounded. You will be notified in writing of the CPS findings.

Unfounded Report

The report is unfounded if the investigation reveals that abuse or neglect did not occur. Unless you desire services, the local social services department will no longer be involved with your family.

A record of the investigation findings will be kept for one year and purged unless there are subsequent reports concerning the same child or you within that year. You may request that the record be kept for up to two additional years.

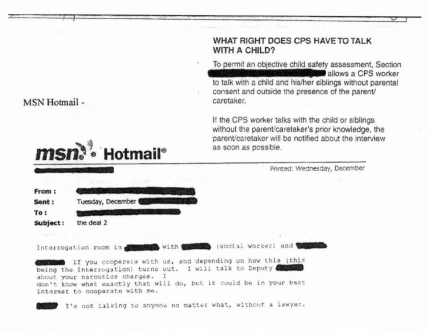

MSN Hotmail -

Printed: Wednesday, December

From :
Sent : Tuesday, December
To :
Subject : the deal 2

Interrogation room in ▓▓▓▓▓ with ▓▓▓▓▓ (social worker) and ▓▓▓▓

▓▓▓▓▓ If you cooperate with us, and depending on how this (this being the interrogation) turns out. I will talk to Deputy ▓▓▓▓ about your narcotics charges. I don't know what exactly that will do, but it could be in your best interest to cooperate with me.

▓▓▓▓▓ I'm not talking to anyone no matter what, without a lawyer.

It was later when I learned more about what transpired during the police "raid on my house." That evening my mother took Iris, my niece, and I to a local production of a play that I'm positive would not have been entertaining on the most mundane of days. I don't know if the rest of the party sincerely agreed that the play was the maximum yawn or they were only deferring to me. As we escaped between the first and second acts, I couldn't even connect with who "me" was. I felt like I was someone else.

C

I think it was around three in the afternoon when Aidan called and told me. It'd been so long since I'd talked to him. I did know that nothing appeared to be happening on the whole thing—either of our "cases"—I had kind of expected my teacher to be back at school any day. Of course, I wouldn't be in class.

After my almost 30 days of suspension, they sent me to an alternative school so I could be involved in a drug program. Goddamned shit is a joke. None of my teachers from the real school send me any work so mostly I just sleep. Then during the drug part we just share our experiences. Man, there are some dumbasses in there. They like to talk like they're the shit, but truthfully they're just wannabe gangsters. I don't know if anything gets on my nerves more than a wigger and his bullshit rap. A couple people are cool though, I usually talk to them when we got our breaks.

I do miss some stuff about school. It is my fucking senior year, I mean. Here it is January and I got another three weeks at this place. So, what the hell? What are they looking for? They already searched my car and my house, talked to some of my friends. It's not like I'm talking on my phone, incriminating myself. Well, if that was next on their list it's too late now. Ditched that fucker on the spot. All this shit is really getting to be too much. Like I don't' have enough of my own shit to deal with.

I know it's partly my fault, but it's not ALL my fault. I didn't know what to say to Aidan. What could I say?

Me: Well, tell your mom I hope she's okay.
A: She's pretty shaken up.
Me: Tell her I love her.
A: I will. Bye, babe.
Me: Bye.
That was it. I mean what could I do?

A

Fucking cops!

Like they really needed to storm the house with 15 uniforms to control one 120 lb woman. Man, thank god Frankie and Barry came to work and told me. And my bosses are cool—they were just like, "No, go."

Jesus! I got home and my mom looks like a prisoner in her own house. Yeah, I just wanted one of those mother fuckers to say something to me—I guess that guy who was, what, guarding my mom?—did stand up (hand on his holster) when I burst in the door, but at that moment I didn't give a shit. So, arrest me for walking in my own front door.

All I could do was hug her. She was crying like she'd been saving tears her whole life. She was telling me, "I'm sorry, baby." She thought it was her fault? I couldn't say much. I had always been a gutsy kid—must have been born with it if all the stories I've heard are true. My mom likes to tell the one about the time in daycare when the teacher tried to punish me by giving me dishwashing soap to drink. I downed the inch in the glass like it was water and said, "Yum, that was good, can I have some more?"

So, my history proved that there could have been a million cops there, and they'd all get treated the same—as one great obstruction to justice. But my mom? My one and only mom? That was a different story altogether. I wanted so bad to take it all away, to tell her positively everything would end and be good. I wanted her to not crumble and give in. I'd been home from Iraq less than six months, and they Army was heavy on soldiers learning not to fear the enemy. But I had learned not to fear the enemy long before the Army. My whole life had taught me not to fear. Now, though, I was afraid. I was afraid my mom was going to let them dissolve her. I was afraid she was slowly disappearing in my arms. And I couldn't stop her.

I missed the whole Frankie and Barry saga from the house. I got the general idea from Barry when they came to get me. Frankie was pretty freaked out—mostly worried that the parents might find out. At the time I wasn't thinking much about what Frankie was saying. All I could focus on was getting home to be with my mom.

Later, when I was clearer, I wondered how Frankie was concerned at all for his situation. I mean, the police let them go. They knew the "green, leafy substance" and the "glass smoking device" didn't belong to my mom, and they still let them go. Maybe Frankie didn't really appreciate what a serious skate that was—not much past interaction with police, apparently. Barry, on the other hand, (like me) couldn't fucking believe it. He said it like this.

On a Friday in January (I think) I, Barry Jackson Smith, was ~~escorted~~ woken up at 11:35 AM by a loud yell and banging at the door. I was hearing someone yelling, "Open up we have a warrent!" I was laying down in the basement when a couple minutes later ~~escape~~ ~~~~ I saw officers coming down the stairs pointing guns and a flashlight saying, "lay face down on the ground and don't move." I followed these instructions while I was then handcuffed. The officers brought me upstairs into the kitchen where I sat and answered questions about myself. Next, i was asked by an officer if there was weed downstairs. I first said no, then the cop ~~s~~ said they found a pipe, and I needed to ~~~~ tell them how much pot was downstairs. Finally, I said there was pot. The pot was downstairs located in a purse that belonged to Frankie Jones, ~~~~ as well as the pipe. I was then told to sit on the couch. I waited for the officer's to let us leave at approx. 1pm. Frankie and I were taken outside where the officer yelled at us that, "He doesn't like being lied to, and myself and Frankie were very close to going to jail." (For lying about the pot) We then were allowed to leave.

Barry J Smith
Barry Jackson Smith

Well, Frankie pretty much had the same experience:

MAiL

Print - Close Window

I woke up to banging on the front door and screaming. Barry and I we laying on the sofa bed trying to figure out what was going on and about ten police officers/investigators stormed downstairs yelling at us to put our hands in the air and to lay face on the ground. They asked if there was anyone else in the basement. I said "I don't think so." I didn't know what time it was and Aiden had gone to work. They had flashlights in our faces so I couldn't see much, but I'm 99% sure they had guns pointed at us. As we were lying on the ground, they cuffed us and brought us upstairs to the kitchen. One officer asked if we sleep over all the time. We said no and then Barry said that he had a few beers and didn't want to drive home. The officer also asked for my name, number, address, and work information and then asked what I had in the basement. I told him my purse and clothes were down there. I had smoked a little pot that night before I went to bed and remembered that I put the rest of it in a bag and then put that bag in my purse. There was only about 1/3 of a gram left. I'm not quite sure exactly where I placed the pipe, but it was either right next to my purse or on top of it. After we had been in the kitchen for about 15 minutes (still cuffed) one of the officers brought me aside and asked if there was anything in the basement that I shouldn't have. He also said "this basement is going to be torn apart. We will find it if it's down there."I said no thinking they weren't going to search my purse. The same officer then brought Barry aside and asked him the same question. He said there might be just a little pot. The officers took our cuffs off and let us sit in the living room while they searched the basement. About 20 minutes later, an officer came upstairs and said that Barry and I were free to go. He walked us outside and then said to me, "You lied to me about the marijuana. We found the pipe too. You're this close to getting a summons, but I'm going to let you go. Don't lie to police; it will only get you in trouble."

I'm willing to do whatever it takes. It was my pot and pipe. I will testify in a heartbeat. I hope this helps ☺

I don't think Frankie realized that their possible arrest was now going to try and be pinned on my mom! I'm not getting down on Frankie—when it came to writing a statement of what really happened, both of them wrote it in a minute. I know they love my mom. All my friends love my mom; none of them would ever consider fucking her over.

But the cops? Totally different, fucking story—different goddamned planet, those assholes are from. Do they think we're morons? Let's see-

Asshole Cop*: (to Frankie) I'm gonna search this bag. This is yours right?

F: Yeah.
AC: Is there anything in there you wanna tell me about now? Before I find it on my own?
F: No.
AC: (Half a second later pulls out a tiny bit of green and a glass bowl) Well, what is this? (Looks back and forth between Frankie and Barry) Anybody?
F: I guess it's mine.
AC: This is your purse, yeah? This is where I found the . . . (Holds the items up) Yeah?
F: Yeah.
AC: Okay, let's go. (Herds him up the stairs)

*   AC is the same as MSC from Willow's transcript.

Next thing you know, those fuckers let Frankie and Barry go free. (I don't know what they could have stuck him with.) Frankie said, "He took us outside in front of the house and said, 'I guess this is your lucky day, but . . . (Stern stare at Frankie) . . . you lied to me.'" After a pause, he ended, "Don't ever lie to the police." AC scanned the immediate vicinity then waved in Barry and Frankie's direction. "Go on, get out of here."

At least they came straight to get me. They were both trying to tell the story at the same time, but in two minutes all I could say was, "So, my mom's there by herself?"

That was it. A split second to my boss's face, 15 seconds for the gist. Negative seconds for him to say, "No, problem, go!"

God, she looked so small, sitting on the couch, doing nothing (not free to do anything) while the house was crawling with power hungry idiots who could care less about her. I know she wouldn't have called me—even if there had been one benevolent soul among the idiots who might have recognized the aura of abandonment around her and asked if there was someone she wanted to call—she probably wouldn't have. She would take all the responsibility and want to save me from being part of it.

The unfortunate part of her position in the situation was that I was way more adept at dealing with the kind of pejorative, authoritative cretinism filling our house at the moment. If I learned nothing else from my turn in the military, I got that there are a considerable number of people in this world who need to exert power over others in order to feel good about themselves. Not like I didn't know it before the Army, but, that day, all around me were ex-military control junkies as far as I'm concerned.

The only half-way decent one there was the token guy. All the assholes were from the neighboring county, so I guess protocol demanded there be a representative from the actual county in which we lived. I suppose I mean "decent" by comparison. I mean he *was* "guarding" us on the couch, but he was pretty laid back and conversational. Yeah, well, at the same time, he had no real vested interest.

Later I thought he was a little casual when he talked about how he had pulled "the duty." He said something like, "I came in this morning and looked at the board. There was like a break-in at some office building and a possible identity theft of some guy who thinks he's a big deal. Then there was *this*. It definitely looked like the most exciting possibility of them all."

W

Are you fucking shitting me? This cop has the nerve to say that he "picked" the assignment of storming my house because it was more exciting than anything else he had to choose from. Yeah, at the time he seemed like the only normal person there and compared to the asshole who claimed that if he'd had to endure our three hours it would be "miller time," I guess this guy looked like a prince . . .

Come on though, how do people get so cavalier about a job that, most times, has such profound effect on those with whom they come in contact. Sure, sure, they get jaded, but I could be the same in my job. I could be a teacher who just decides that all kids are the same, and I don't try anymore. If that ever became my perspective I would have to move on to something else. I don't understand how people justify some of the shit they do. I suppose I could accept stuff like what my brother tells me about why lawyers are like they are. (He is a lawyer, after all.) He says because it's in the Constitution—everyone deserves representation in the courts. It makes no difference whether the attorney believes his/her client. No matter, if there are dated videotapes showcasing said client committing the heinous crime, regardless of a shit ton of legitimate incriminating evidence, every person deserves equal representation under our set of laws.

Okay, that only means to me that there are going to be some unscrupulous attorneys or attorneys who are able to segregate their personal code of ethics from their task. I guess I can't do that. I could never adequately represent a person who I believed to be guilty of the crime—maybe a nebulous or inconsequential or (stupid) crime—a crime that's only a crime because the law against it is ridiculous. For instance, a person who steals food to feed starving children, or a father who attacks, maims, kills the man who raped and murdered his 5 year-old daughter, I could probably do back flips with the law in cases like that.

Well, those situations are few and far between. For the majority of the time, most people in positions of any power lord it over those they are "above." What is wrong with this whole creation? How can humans display such fresh intelligence in certain ways (medicine, technology, architecture) and remain so appallingly stale in others (personal growth, relationships, introspection)? I see so few individuals who ever recognize this, much less care about it.

My house was full of such a type on that day. As they filed out the door with envelopes, papers, folders and boxes, it seemed so twisted that the law sworn to protect could burst into a citizen's house, scoop up a subjective list of his/her personal belongings and march out without an explanatory word.

No, there were a few words. Adolph, the lead detective on the case handed me two sheets of paper as he was leaving. It was an itemized list of what they had taken. Aidan stood right next to me as I reordered the papers so that the first page was on top. Aidan and I started at the beginning and stopped. The first two items listed were a "bag of green leafy substance" and "glass smoking device".

We spoke in unison, "Wait a minute, those aren't ours."

Adolph wouldn't make eye contact. "No one said they were yours. This is just a list of items we took from your house." He moved toward the front door as he spoke, so calm, so assured, so unfeeling . . .

Aidan followed him. "You know your guys took that off someone else." He said it so fearlessly. "Remember, then you let them go."

Adolph didn't acknowledge the fact in any way. He and the remnants of his crew strolled out the door purposefully—with a commitment equal to the manner in which they had arrived.

Aidan was fabulous. I was a wreck. I can't think of a time when I had ever before been so completely unable to function. My house, what was my sanctuary, had been carelessly and callously invaded.

Here is the complete list of the items they removed. I've typed Adolph's wording exactly. My commentary is in parentheses.

Search inventory and return

1. GLASS SMOKING DEVICE (Frankie's)
2. BAG OF GREEN LEAFY SUBSTANCE (Frankie's)
3. E-MACHINES TOWER (computer from kitchen)
4. 2 PICTURE CDS (family and friends)
5. 1 PICTURE CD (family and friends)
6. BAG CONTAINING 74 PHOTOS & 1 CD (Aidan's)
7. 2006 WEEKLY PLANNER (used for Willow's pt job w/a realtor)
8. DIGITAL CAMERA (used for Willow's pt job w/a realtor)
9. 35 MM ROLL OF FILM (Nicolina's)
10. 2 PARTY INVITATIONS & 4 ADDRESS STICKERS (invitations from Willow's Housewarming—5 years old and Willow's '70's Party—1 year old. Labels could be anything: for Christmas cards, Aidan's various military addresses, Willow's return address, agents and publishers, ex-husband . . .)
11. E-MACHINES TOWER (computer from basement—not used in 3 years)
12. DELL THUMBDRIVE (Aidan's)
13. 4 CDS, 2 JOURNALS, 53 3.5 FLOPPY DISKS (Aidan's CDs and journals, Willow's disks—mostly school projects, tests, quizzes and lesson plans)
14. TELE-RECORDER CONTAINING 1 TAPE (about 10 years old, the only recording on the tape is a phone call from Adolph—ironic, don't you think?)
15. BURNED CD, TITLE: CAINE'S SOUNDTRACK (Aidan's)
16. 5 PHOTOS FROM REFRIGERATOR (I only remember 3, no idea about the other 2)
17. SAMSUNG CELL PHONE (Willow's brand new birthday present from Phoebe)
18. PAPER WITH NAMES AND PHONE NUMBERS (Phoebe's)
19. 3 MISCELLANEOUS NOTES (no idea. if you've read to this point, you see that we are a family of "note writers")
20. BURNED CD, TITLE: VALENTINE'S DAY MIX (Aidan made for Willow)
21. LETTERS, TOP RIGHT DRAWER, MASTER BEDROOM (from Willow's ex-husband)
22. LETTERS, TOP LEFT DRAWER, MASTER BEDROOM (from Willow's ex-boyfriend)
23. PICTURES, BOTTOM CENTER DRAWER, MASTER BATHROOM (no idea. Willow's ex-boyfriend?)
24. LETTERS, CLOSET, MASTER BEDROOM (no idea—just must be old)

25. PHOTOS, CLOSET, MASTER BEDROOM (definitely very old)
26. MOTOROLA CELL PHONE (Aidan's)
27. MICROCASSETTE TAPE (no idea—very old)
28. GROW A DATE NOVELTY GIFT* (see note below)
29. 3 CDS WITH PHOTOS (family and friends—very old)

* The confiscation of GROW A DATE was both maddeningly unfathomable and hysterically amusing. Basically, it is a little, red, three-dimensional, rubber-like man. About three inches tall, once submerged in water, it "grows" to about six inches. I received this NOVELTY GIFT from a **female** student my second year of teaching as a Christmas gift. She was constantly trying to "hook me up" with other single teachers at our school. When I review paragraph #3 from the Affidavit for Search Warrant which describes, "things . . . to be searched for . . . ," I find no relevant category aside from "sexual enhancement instruments." I realize you don't know me, but I am not the type for such "instruments." Notice that there is nothing else on the list which remotely falls under such a heading.

I ask you. Is this evidence of deviancy? GROW A DATE?

CAINE LEAVES
THE GARDEN

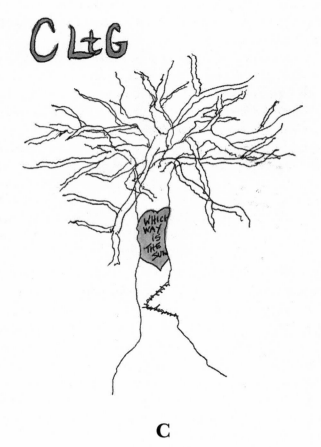

C

I can't handle this shit anymore. It's all gotten so complicated.

I really don't give a fuck about the police and what they think. I mean, come on, so they find pictures in my car from some random hotel party, and they want to pin that on Willow and Aidan? They question some of the people in the pictures as if the pictures were taken at anyone's house. Do the fucking cops not know what a hotel room looks like? And, ohmigod, how much police training did it take for them to be able to track down the people from the photos? Gee, let's see, um, go to school and show the pics to the on-site deputy? Shit, there's some serious detective work.

So, I IM'ed one of the girls I know the police talked to. That's how I know they can't tell a real house from a hotel, and they're asking her all this shit about where she parties and if she knows teachers who party . . . whatever.

What pissed me off the most is how they act like I don't know what the fuck is up. What did they say, wait, something like, ok, she asked why they wanted to know all of what they were asking, and dickhead says something like, "We think something bad happened to this boy, but the boy doesn't know it's bad." What the fuck?! What am I? A moron? Jesus, I hate cops.

The worst thing is that I don't even know **how** I feel anymore. It's weird how you can be so into something at one point and then so out of it so fast . . .

I've always thought about a lot of shit . . . all the time . . . ever since I can remember. But somewhere along the line I got the idea that it wasn't a good thing or maybe there was just no one who wanted to hear it or could understand it.

I don't know why that occurs to me now. I thought I'd gotten used to it . . . fuck, I don't even know how to describe it anymore ~ if I ever did. There was a time when stuff seemed easier. Like in middle school I got A's in everything without even thinking. I know I didn't think about school back then caz my head was always full of all the other shit I was thinking about. Like plans, inventions, ways around stuff, picturing different ways to end at the same point, imagining how many possible outcomes there might be for some random person's life . . .

And it all happened in a way that I can't describe. All my thoughts traveled at warp speed, but I **knew** them all. Maybe that's why I could never say them to anyone so they could understand ~ like they couldn't keep up.

I guess I got tired . . . frustrated. After I got to high school . . . I'd lost weight, learned to manage my charisma . . . it was a whole different story. And there were girls . . . and drugs.

They say drugs are an escape and that's bad, but what if it's better than what you have? I can't say there was one day when I **decided** drugs were helpful. I don't know even that I realized or thought about it before now. You know how it goes, one thing leads to another.

I guess I'm only thinking about it now because I can't or don't want to deal with the way all this current shit has turned out. I know it's bad for everybody. Shit, Ms. Kincaid lost her job. I can't talk to Aidan or anyone for that matter ~ I'm grounded, no phone, don't go to "real" school anymore.

I just need a break. I can't go back to that kid whose thoughts were out of control. I can't change or fix anything that's happened.

I have to move on.

Goddamnit, I'm not tryin' to just dip . . . like I don't care, but what choice do I have? It's my fucking senior year, and I've been suspended more days then I've actually been there. Now I'm going to this joke of an "alternative" school, not learning jack . . . I just want the fuck out of here.

So, "the **boy** doesn't know it's bad"? They act like I'm a child. Am I? Well, if so, then this child knows enough to know that his involvement in this situation needs to end . . . for everyone's sake.

I really hope they understand.

FAMILY STORM

W

It's not like I didn't need or want my family. I wasn't trying to keep my suspension a secret. As I've said, I thought every day it was going to be over.

It was about two weeks after it happened. One of Aidan's friends had stopped by but Aidan wasn't home. I chatted with the guy for a few minutes when the doorbell rang. Either it was kind of late or I was just growing increasingly paranoid (I know I wasn't expecting anyone), but I immediately felt nervous.

Aidan's friend was leaving so he walked to the door with me. On the front porch were my mother and one of my brothers.

I don't remember a lot of details, and I didn't write down what happened with them . . . maybe I should have because even today, as I recall that night, it makes me feel bad. I think my mom asked, "Willow, what's going on?" (So right away, I knew they knew.)

Aidan's friend definitely felt the vibe. I could see it in his eyes and feel it when he hugged me good-bye.

So my mom tells me that a friend of hers (who is also the parent of a couple of my students) told **her** that I wasn't working. I remember feeling accused, guilty already.

I told them in a nutshell:

> I'm too friendly with students (apparently one in particular)
> A certain administrator doesn't like me (my mom knew that already)
> Caine just happened to be my student **and** a friend of Aidan's.

I explained as much as I could without betraying anyone and keeping in mind my attorney's moratorium on my talking **AT ALL, TO ANYONE**.

I think (I think) that by the time they left they were acting supportively, but I remember the interaction to this day as one in which I had been judged before I even had the opportunity to explain . . . kind of like the way I've realized our whole system is . . .

My family thought I was guilty until proven innocent.

NOTES BETWEEN
AIDAN AND WILLOW

Mother,
You ARE AN exceptional human being.
I ♡ you so much. I will be
here when you get home faum. The
tatoo touch up was painful. → It looks
good though. Have A FABULOUS DAY @
school.

♡ Aidan

Aidan—
I love you! I'll miss you!
Be good. Enjoy responsibly.
(that's just a commercial — not me)

I'll call you tonight.

♡ Mom

Please have the house looking the same as
it does now when we get back.
Thank you, honey.

ISOLATION REALIZED

I tried in the beginning. I can't stress enough how I thought it would all be cleared up, how I kept thinking that for so long . . . too long, I guess. I think I said that it probably took "The Invasion" before it really hit me that my situation was pretty fucking serious. Yes, Ray and Diana (especially Diana) had told me, how it was, had been, continued to be . . . with cases like mine . . . WITH SO MANY CASES LIKE MINE, but I (unconsciously, I guess) persisted in believing that qualities like truth, faith and love would win. I still can't believe, with all the life experience I have had—abandonment and neglect as a child, suffering through catastrophic results of my poor marriage decisions, perpetual financial disaster and years of therapy, that I persisted in believing in my heart.

These are emails I sent to teachers in my department within the two weeks following my suspension. If I received a response, it is included here, but these represent the total of my communication with what was so much of my life. After these, there was nothing.

From: Willow Kincaid
To: ██████
Date: Thursday - December ████
Subject: Tricks

██████

I just wanted to let you know that I will be out of school for a little while. I am fine, but I have some things to do and don't know when I'll be back.
██████ told me you are opting out of the mentoring program at semester (like you needed mentoring anyway), but I am still available to help you if you have a question or want any materials... stuff like that. I know you have ██, and he is great so I'm not worried. If you could just send me an email now and then just to keep me up with where you are that would be great. Also, thanks for any help you are already giving my 11th grade.
Have a wonderful day!

Willow

From: Willow Kincaid
To: ██████
Date: Thursday - December ████
Subject: a stranger among us

██████

Do me a favor, please, and remind the following people that this woman, ██████ is coming to observe them teach on the following dates:
12/████ (1, 2 & 3)
12/████ (5, 7 & 8)
12/████ (1, 2 & 3)
12/████ (8) She needs a 7th period to observe on this day. It was supposed to be me, but maybe she can see ██ or ██ instead.

I told her to sign in and then come to the workroom around 8:45. Maybe ██ can plan to be down there on Monday to retrieve her.

Thanks for your help. Let me know if you need more info.

Willow

From: Willow Kincaid
To: ██████
Date: Thursday - December ████
Subject: the state of the union

Hey, ██████

I wanted you to know that I will be out of school for a little while. I am fine, but I don't know when I'll be back. You probably know that you are eligible to opt out of the mentoring program at semester if you want. I'm not encouraging you to do that. I want you to know that I will still help you as much as I can...even if it's just to talk about what a horrendous workload you have :). Let me know. It's really no imposition to me (actually gives me something to do), but if it's annoying to you to have to write one more email, I understand.
You are doing a fabulous job, by the way.
Good luck at the pep rally!

Willow

From: **Willow Kincaid**
To: ▮
Date: Thursday - December ▮
Subject: Tricks

▮

I just wanted to let you know that I will be out of school for a little while. I am fine, but I have some things to do and don't know when I'll be back.
▮ told me you are opting out of the mentoring program at semester (like you needed mentoring anyway), but I am still available to help you if you have a question or want any materials... stuff like that. I know you have ▮, and he is great so I'm not worried. If you could just send me an email now and then just to keep me up with where you are that would be great. Also, thanks for any help you are already giving my 11th grade.
Have a wonderful day!

Willow

From: **Willow Kincaid**
To: ▮
Date: Thursday - December ▮
Subject: a stranger among us

▮

Do me a favor, please, and remind the following people that this woman, ▮ is coming to observe them teach on the following dates:
12/▮ (1,2 & 3)
12/▮ (5, 7 & 8)
12/▮ (1, 2 & 3)
12/▮ (8) She needs a 7th period to observe on this day. It was supposed to be me, but maybe she can see ▮ or ▮ instead.

I told her to sign in and then come to the workroom around 8:45. Maybe ▮ can plan to be down there on Monday to retrieve her.

Thanks for your help. Let me know if you need more info.
Willow

From: **Willow Kincaid**
To: ▮
Date: Thursday - December ▮
Subject: the state of the union

Hey, ▮
I wanted you to know that I will be out of school for a little while. I am fine, but I don't know when I'll be back. You probably know that you are eligible to opt out of the mentoring program at semester if you want. I'm not encouraging you to do that. I want you to know that I will still help you as much as I can...even if it's just to talk about what a horrendous workload you have :). Let me know. It's really no imposition to me (actually gives me something to do), but if it's annoying to you to have to write one more email, I understand.
You are doing a fabulous job, by the way.
Good luck at the pep rally!
Willow

From:	Willow Kincaid
To:	████████
Date:	Friday - December ████
Subject:	Re: how it's going

*

████

Let me know what kind of project you decided on for The Pearl. I always love new projects. Also, I have a binder on my desk in the workroom (I think it's yellow), anyway, it says "WRITING" on the spine. Feel free to look through it and see if anything looks useful to you.
You're doing a great job! Thank you.

Willow

████████████████████████

Hi Willow

I'm sorry to hear that you will be out for a while. Thank you for wanting to stay in touch-I would love to. The classes are busy finishing up The Pearl right now, and I am reviewing grammar at the same time. We will transition into writing after winter break. (The students have been writing all year, but we will continue to improve it-I hope). I will certainly keep you updated on how things are going.

Take Care!

████

████████████████████████

Hey, ████
Just wanted to send you a note and tell you that I am going to be out of school for a little while. I am fine, but I have some things to take care of. (I know, you're not supposed to end a sentence with a preposition.)
I do want to stay in touch with you while I'm out, though. If you could just let me know how it's going every once in a while, if you need anything. I still want to help you as best I can.
Have a great day!

Willow

I don't blame anyone. Although I take responsibility for everything that has transpired since that day in December, I don't accept blame. I never did anything wrong, and I hope you see that.

But I completely lost myself for months. I don't think anyone can fully understand what that means unless he or she has experienced it. I'll try and tell you what it feels like. It is like, "The Staircase Which Only Descends."

It's like a thousand bags of sand settling inside you, but at the same time it comes in the guise of that unthreatening snowfall—people of the cold know that the swirling, glorious, recognizable flakes portend transcendence, it's the particle-imitating rain of snow that endures . . . and endures.

That's how this comes. Deceptively showering innocence, it is internalized as "just the way it goes." Then, so savagely hardening into brutality~ a shell forms ~ which is now the skeleton of all immediate possibilities.

How does this phantom know every single ingredient for a crushing recipe? How is it that every lost prize joins with every word of rejection and any possible doubt links to any imaginable failure?

Why does it have to be so completely complete?

It doesn't matter if the staircase is abysmal or the sun is arrogant. The prize could be unremarkable, the love unrequited, the choice miniscule, the future paranoid, but the sincerity of direction remains constant.

Down, down, down . . .

Sometimes . . . any moment prior to oblivion, . . . these questions battle in "logical" defense, but they are less than the revered speed of light in the face of an undiscovered infinity bursting into invisibility.

The sadness is the worst. Guilt, shame, regret . . . they can be reconciled, but . . . inexplicable sadness . . . that's what settles, endures, hardens and paralyzes.

My only reason for living says, "Walk like you mean it," and I cry.

Sometime in March, before the "Good News (?)" section at the end of this book, it all hit me, how far gone I was. I had a conversation with someone. It was one of those times when, in the course of talking, you, yourself, say the profound words you need to hear. It was emotional, and what I said was, "I just want myself back."

He said, "I want yourself back, too."

I can't begin to tell you how hard it is to do. I can't give you instructions to follow in case it ever happens to you. I can't cite any resources I consulted. All I can give you (aside from everything I have written so far) is a particular realization I had. I call it The 5% Philosophy.

THE PHILOSOPHY

THE 5

You can't fully appreciate the 1% unless it (they) are juxtaposed to the 5%. Or maybe you can, I wouldn't know, I'm not in that fraction. You could read the end of this first, then tell me if you even needed all this. Whatever you do will be best.

(5%) INDICATIONS —

Reject authority in all it's forms.

the term "professional" means nothing w/o actual demonstration

Difficulties in school are due to a general interpretation of the material as "pointless." (often "honor" level performance disappears after MS — parents, teachers, "We don't understand. What happened?")

Often told how much POTENTIAL you have —

LABELS: OCD   ANTI-SOCIAL
ADD   EMO
ADHD

Believe that knowing a little bit about a lot of things is preferable to knowing a lot about one thing.

PRONE 2 EXTREMES — positive + negative

Emotions, Relationships, Addictions, Activities, BUT all easily interchangeable

Unmotivated for anything without a clear and meaningful outcome.*

*outcomes could just be internally felt and attempting to articulate your rationale to most others is frustrating.

CAN UNDERSTAND SUICIDE ~ thought about it.

(ALWAYS) felt different

Generally NOT passive aggressive

Generally considered physically attractive by more people than not.

ALWAYS KNEW YOU WERE SUPPOSED TO DO SOMETHING BUT DON'T KNOW WHAT IT IS.

I f *Tragic Hero: A Teacher Accused (ONE)* has held your attention, you might want to read Book Two when it comes out. In Book Two, The 5% Philosophy is fully explained. For now, I can only give you the overview and impetus.

Well, the impetus was completely the hell into which I was unwittingly thrust, but I'm not going to at all say that I accepted, incorporated, recovered or survived any of it easily. I said it from the start, and I'll say it again, "THIS HAS BEEN HELL!" (And that doesn't even feel sufficient.) After a couple months of not working but getting paid, it was mentioned to me that I was "lucky." The first time the concept was even intimated to me, I thought I might spontaneously combust. I don't know. Maybe I overreacted all along, but even in retrospect (even a year later) I feel how severe the battle was. So many aspects of my life changed so drastically, and every single part that changed felt like molten lead in my veins. Let me provide some illustration. I am a teacher, for gods' sakes. These are just a few of the "side effects" from my ordeal. I give no explanation for these ~ only for The Philosophy.

I had worked out daily (running and weight training) since my teens. I stopped.

I had never taken any regular medication. I had three prescriptions.

I hadn't eaten at a fast food establishment since high school. I started to think it didn't matter.

I had gotten up at 5:30 a.m. for at least the previous 10 years. I started waking up at 2 in the afternoon.

I had weighed around 135 for years. My weight dropped to 120.

I had meditated for 15 years on a fairly daily basis. I stopped.

I had always been complimented on my fingernails; they always grew like crazy and were strong. My nails barely grew for months and when they did, broke immediately.

I present all of the preceding because I want you to know how devastating something inside you can be to the outside of you. I didn't MEAN to change all of what changed. It's like I didn't even realize it was changing until it was already gone . . . until a new, different habit had consumed me. Even now, now that I've recovered myself to a certain place, this is very hard to write.

Let me give "The 5% Philosophy" overview instead.

Indications of the 5%

1. **Reject authority in all its forms**
2. **Difficulties completing academic requirements in school**

   —often honor students until late Middle School or early High School
   —academics come so easily it seems pointless, so it doesn't get done OR
   —the work is so easily completed there is no thought about it

3. Often told how much "potential" they have in the context of insinuating that they aren't living up to it
4. Completely committed to anything they find personally captivating—activity, person, thought process

   —almost painful to perform any task without explained and agreed upon relevancy to their lives

5. Feeling their whole lives (no matter how long) that they are somehow different from most other people
6. Lack of trust in "professionals"—media, medicine, law . . .
7. Exhibit addictive tendencies . . . not just to substances but emotions, lifestyles, individuals . . .

   —particular attraction to "risk"—from extreme danger to borderline poor-house-type debt (often for unnecessary items)
   —extremes of any kind, also at the other end of the spectrum: phobias, isolation, neediness
   —tendencies usually freely conveyed to others (who seem interested), accompanied by a detailed rationale (for those who seem interested)

8. Easily obsessed with ANYTHING, but minutely able to switch obsessions to something completely different
9. Generally believe that knowing a little bit about a lot of things is preferable to knowing a lot about one thing
10. Often diagnosed by some "authority" as ADD, ADHD, OCD or ODD

    —caveat: don't exhibit the attention deficits in areas of interest
    —caveat: usually OCD about something specific—order, hygiene, food, routine (not all)
    —overall caveat: generally accepting of their personal proclivity, doubt occurs only as a result of others' responses to it
    —even w/o the diagnosis of attention deficit, they must exert effort to stay focused on what they consider to be meaningless to their own perspective
    —also, change activities frequently (whenever the current one ceases to have relevance to the moment)

11. Strong aversion toward particular majority earmarks: social ills, philosophies, etc. (any issue without logical support)

—list grows over time commensurate with increased depth of logic

—laisse-faire on other issues which would seem to be similar (they might reject a prevailing mindset but wouldn't fight over it)

12. Inherently self-reflective
13. 100% motivated only by what exhibits a clear and meaningful outcome

—the "result" could just be a personal, internal knowledge of expected satisfaction

—VERY OFTEN the sense that others don't understand their inability to articulate their personal rationales

—the above attempts to explain frequently result in frustration

14. They can understand the concept of suicide in ANY form

—have considered it themselves

15. Usually KNOW the best way for others to communicate information to them (draw a picture, act it out, create an analogy, etc.), but don't feel supported in asking for it
16. Have a highly intuitive sense of humor, most often expressed stringently in one of two extremes

—sarcasm, wry comments . . .

—methodically planned practical jokes

17 Always. Fairly to very physically attractive
18. Trouble choosing a career. Change jobs often. (the Japanese?)
19. Creative in many mediums, but one generally takes precedence (in interest or ability)
20. Have always known they are supposed to DO SOMETHING in their lives. If feels important, but they don't know what it is.

NOTES TO THE READER:

The #1 way to recognize another of the 5% (only, of course, if you are one yourself, but you wouldn't have possession of this information in this format if you weren't) is through your own senses. If you feel as close as you can be to SURE that you have identified another like you, try this (CAUTIOUSLY):

Begin to explain however much it is you know about us. Anyone truly part of the 5 will not doubt for a second, any questions he/she asks will likely be the same ones for which we have limited answers. Be careful about taking the step of introducing this "philosophy" to others. Beginning our explanation should only be undertaken when your whole self has felt the familiar vibrations from another for a significant period of time (of course, "significant" is personally relative—like all your perspective). What should happen over your own significant period is an ever—expanding sense that, not only is the other person a part of us, but you KNOW he/she NEEDS to hear about it. Just . . .

REMEMBER: This list of indications is not all-inclusive, and neither is any combination of traits mutually-exclusive.

Finally, there is this VERY IMPORTANT POINT. A true member of the 5% will always react to the explanation in a manner similar to this:

—attentive, rarely interrupting, eager to hear but calm (definitely no cheerleader reactions) able to comment on or question any of your explanation intelligently, QUITE OFTEN your overwhelming sense from the other person will be the relief he/she feels at the news. Usually the interaction between you ends with his/her verbal acknowledgement and some statement reflective of his/her past attempts to apply a semblance of this knowledge to his/her own experience.

THE REGULARS
SUPPORT GROUP

L ike I said, you can get more information about how this all came about from Book Two of Tragic Hero. Really, I'd give it all to you now, but I am so tired. Writing this manuscript has been like reliving it all over again, and I badly want to get to "The Good News (?)."

Notes and Games

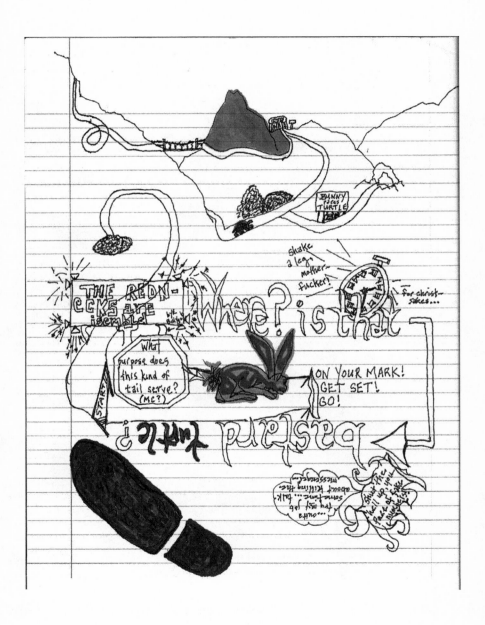

Live

Quality
of Albums

Italian opera
*Andrea Bocelli
→ Love the singing
→ Don't know a word
of Italian
Musical's & Opera
*Andrew Lloyd Webber
→ Phantom of the Opera
- Music of the Night √+
* Julie Andrews
→ Sound of Music
- Do ray me fa (title?)

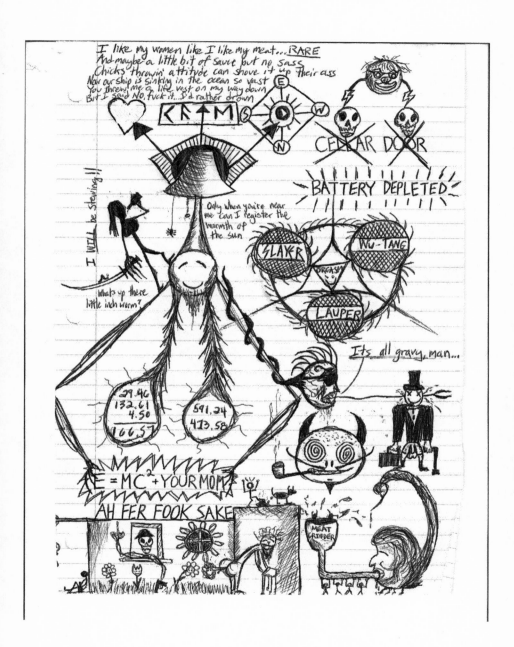

Hey momma! I totally forgot that my car is still at RTC. I walked up to get some coffee. call me when you get up so I can bum a ride :i Thanks.
Love you!

DEAR ~~Roxanne~~

I NEED A JOB . . . . ~~████~~
NANCY FANCY IS MY NEW SEXY . . .
I FEEL HER LOVE EVERY WHERE . . .

~~PAPPITA~~

Thanks for the bed ~~treet~~ under which I slept.
12/cc

I LOVE YOU Willow!!

hello beautiful~
I got you
good Jorge
night
2010

Have a good memorial day
र९ु

Thanks for everything !!
♥

Love you Willow! you're the best. Thank you for havin you. ♥

— sunshine

Aidan,
went to doctor's app. I'll call you after.

Barry

Thanks Willow! You're awesome!
See you soon!

Mucho love to you
— Mucho thank you for last Night, I'll see you tonight!
— Jackson

I told you J-Zigga would eat that chocolate covered apple.

I love you mom!
— Aidan

The Regulars ⭐

** First of all, The Regulars ⭐ is a home, so treat it like one. No one is getting paid to host these "get togethers" so we all have to help to keep this place fun. That's the reason everyone likes to come and wants to be a regular.

Here are the guidelines:

1. YOU DO NOT TALK ABOUT THE REGULARS

2. YOU DO NOT TALK ABOUT THE REGULARS

3. Make up your bed, or wherever the f*** you sleep at night whenever you wake up and get ready to leave.

4. Throw away your trash once you make it, that way no one has to clean up your goddamned mess, we are all adults here I think we can handle it.

5. If you make any kind of mess and don't know how to clean it up, what to do, or are just plain embarrassed about how drunk you are and what you did; tell someone, get some help and take care of it. Don't just leave it and hope no one says anything because we will.

6. If you ever need/want something, don't just take it, ask. You might not get the answer you want, but at least we won't have to have you executed for helping yourself.

7. Empty full ashtrays! It takes two seconds, and it helps reduce the mess. Even if you just think the ashtray is sort of full or maybe getting close, empty it.

8. If you use a dish (or any other flatware) rinse and leave in the sink. It's just that simple.

9. Last but not least, the cat is crazy. Do not let her escape. If she does just let someone know.

Funny, it is leaving me now. I am forgetting. It's sad, but I don't cry anymore for how it happened. I cry for the loss of the part that was real but had to be jettisoned along with the rest.

I don't know what can and can't be resurrected in relationships. I only know that it would for damn sure be work ~ both parties would have to WANT to try . . .

. . . but, before we get to the end . . . this next part is crucial . . .

Changing Teams

There would have to be a clear and honest understanding about EXACTLY what part of the relationship was worth restoration. (I can hardly type through these tears . . .)

IN MARCH I GOT
THE GOOD NEWS?

H ere's what it was . . . well, this first document was just included in the file and hardly the "good news," but I thought you might want to see it.

December

Ms. Willow Kincaid
100 Percent Way
Anyone, Anywhere.

RE: Child Protective Service Investigation
    Child Name . Came Blaise.

Dear Ms. Kincaid

I am writing to inform you that ____the____ Department of Social Services received a sexual abuse complaint involving : Came Blaise. ∟ I will be contacting people who may have information pertaining to the investigation. Please contact me to arrange a date for an interview.

Also please be notified that if you choose not to meet with me the investigation will continue and a finding will be made on the evidence available to me. You will be notified of the results upon conclusion of the investigation. Your cooperation in this process is greatly appreciated.

Please find enclosed A Guide to Child Protective Services.

Sincerely.

Child Protective Services Worker

I've included portions of "A Guide to Protective Services" for your information and my own love of irony. Don't misunderstand, I think the premise of the organization is stellar, it's just that so much of the information is completely subjective and situational, and, of course, in my case . . . well, I don't feel as if I should ever have had to interact with them at all.

About Children
and
Their Families

A GUIDE TO CHILD PROTECTIVE SERVICES

WHY HAS A CHILD PROTECTIVE SERVICES (CPS) WORKER CONTACTED ME?

You have been contacted because the department of social services has received a report of possible abuse or neglect of your child(ren) or a child in your care.

Local social services departments are required by law to:

- respond to valid reports of suspected child maltreatment

- assess child safety

- support and preserve families, when possible

- prevent the re(occurrence) of abuse or neglect.

WHAT IS CHILD ABUSE AND NEGLECT?

Section ▓▓▓▓▓▓▓▓▓▓▓▓▓▓▓ defines an abused or neglected child as any child under 18 whose parent or other person responsible for the child's care:

- causes or threatens to cause a nonaccidental physical or mental injury

- neglects or refuses to provide adequate food, clothing, shelter, emotional nurturing, or health care

- abandons the child

- fails to provide adequate supervision in relation to the child's age and level of development

- commits or allows to be committed any illegal sexual act upon a child including incest, rape, fondling, indecent exposure, prostitution, or allows a child to be used in any sexually explicit visual material

WHY WOULD SOMEONE MAKE A REPORT?

The purpose of reporting is to identify abused and neglected children as soon as possible so that their safety and well-being can be ensured. Some signs that people notice and may report are:

- a child who has questionable injuries

- a young child who is left alone

- a child who has unattended health care problems or medical needs

- a child who is consistently hungry or appears malnourished

- a child who has a sexually transmitted disease or other signs of sexual abuse.

Investigation Response

A child abuse or neglect investigation is conducted when there are immediate child safety concerns, previous reports of abuse or neglect, or the report is required by law to be investigated.

Examples include, but are not limited to, reports of:

- sexual abuse

WHO MADE THE REPORT?

Anyone may make a report of suspected child abuse or neglect; however, under ▓▓▓▓ law, professionals and persons who provide services or care for children are required to immediately report their suspicions.

A person who makes a report is not required to provide his/her name. The name of the reporter, if provided, may be released with a Court order or during court testimony.

Okay, the following handwritten section of the "complaint" is included because (as an English teacher) I completely object to the way the punctuation was misconstrued in the typed version which comes after.

NATURE OF COMPLAINT		
ABUSE/NEGLECT CATEGORY Sex abuse		CHILD FATALITY (Y/N) N

Teacher on Admin Leave.

Teacher alleged to have had sexual relationship
w/student. Alleged to have written graphic letter.
Teacher was calling house.

Got ████ on dru/bust. His cell phone went off. She
(teacher) textmsg. w/her phone #. *How many days in a row
we can have sex, how long.*

Referral Narrative Screen Information

What are the details of the alleged abuse/neglect of the children?
Teacher is alleged to have had sexual relationship w/student. Alleged to have written graphic letter. Teacher was calling house. ██████████████████████████████ (Caine.) on drug bust, his cell phone went off -teacher was text messaging him w/her phone# - "How many days in a row we can have sex, how long".

When was the child last seen and by whom? What was the child's condition?

Where are the children located now and how long will they be there? (Include Address and County)

Safety Factors

Who else was told or knows of the situation?

Why are you calling Today

Additional Information:

Does the child have injuries now? If so, describe the injuries?

What are the Risk Factors in the Home? (Domestic Violence, Safety Hazards, Physically/Mentally Disabled Victim, Etc?

E. Abuse/Neglect Information

Alleged Victim Name	Caine Blaise	Death N	Needs Medical Attention N
Substance Abuse Indicated	N	Type	
Abuse Neglect Category	Sexual Abuse	Type	
Alleged by Complainant or Collected during Investigation ?		Alleged by Reporter	

Age of Injury   Injury Characteristics
Injury Locations
Injury Specifics

Abuse/Neglect Specifics

Alleged Abuser/ Neglector   Willow Kincaid
Comments

Referral Information Report
(INTAKE)

Family Name: High School

A. Assignment Information

Date Received	Time Received	Referral Number	Referral Status
December	05:00:00 PM		Valid

Received By		Locality	
██████████			

Referral Transferred to	Locality	Date	Time

Response Type	Referral Status	Validation Date	Screened Out Reason(s)
Out of Family	Valid	December	

Response Priority	Low

Reason for Response Priority Change

Agency Referrals
Recommendations

B. Household Information

Address

Directions

Home Phone #   Work Phone #   ( )   -
Message #

C. Referral Client Information

Name	Gender	DOB/Age	Race	Role in Referral
Caine Blaige E-C	Male	17	White	Alleged Victim
			White	Caretaker
Willow Kincaid	Female	47	White	Alleged Abuser/Neglector

Date	Time	Type of Interaction	Name(s)
January		CONTACT	Ray O'Hanlon Attorney for Ms. Kincaid

Type/Location Telephone   **Status** Completed

Purpose
Case Consultation
Information/Referral

Comments
Worker left a message for Mr. O'Hanlon to call worker.

Date	Time	Type of Interaction	Name(s)
January	4:40 PM	CONTACT	Ray O'Hanlon Attorney for Ms. Kincaid

Type/Location Telephone   **Status** Completed

Purpose
Case Consultation
Information/Referral

Comments
Worker advised Mr. O'Hanlon an that the record could not be released. Worker explained that when there is a criminal case that involves the same victim child and the same alleged abuser for the same alleged abuse then access to the file is not available until after the criminal proceedings are completed. Mr. O'Hanlon stated that he is representing Ms. ▓▓▓ through the teaches association and that Diana de Fiamma is representing Ms. ▓▓▓ in the criminal case. Mr. O'Hanlon stated that Ms. ▓▓▓ has been advised by counsel not to speak with CPS.

Date	Time	Type of Interaction	Name(s)
January 5		RISK ASSESSMENT	Caine Blaise

Risk Level No Reasonably Assessable Risk

Family Name: High School   **Local DSS:** County

Narratives

Date	Time	Type of Interaction	Name(s)
Dec.		Initial Assessment	N/A
Dec.	5:00 pm	Victim Interview	Caine Blaise by Det. Adolph, Police
Dec.		Caretaker Interview	Willow Kincaid
Jan.		Caretaker Interview	Willow Kincaid
Jan.		Contact	Ray O'Hanlon, attorney for Willow Kincaid in civil case
Jan.		Contact	O'Hanlon, attorney for Ms. Kincaid
Jan.	4:40 pm	Contact	" "
Jan.		Risk Assessment	Caine Blaise
Jan.		Contact	Ray O'Hanlon, attorney for Ms. Kincaid in civil case
Feb.		Needs Assessment	Caine Blaise
March		Findings	UNFOUNDED

Date	Time	Type of Interaction	Name(s)
December		INITIAL ASSESSMENT	N/A

Overall Outcome Safe

Ways to show your children that you care

· Notice them

· Ask them about themselves

· Play with them

· Read aloud together

· Hug them

· Praise more

· Suggest better behaviors when they act out

· Criticize less.

tmail -

WHAT ARE MY CHILD'S RIGHTS?

All children have the need and right to be nurtured and live safely in their homes. They have the right to:

· food, clothing, and shelter

· education and health care

· love, acceptance, and positive attention

· protection and freedom from harm or neglect.

:mail®

Printed: Friday, December

From :
Sent :   Tuesday, December
To :
Subject :   what the hell ms ????

Hey what is happening, you've been gone for almost 2 weeks, no one will tell us what happened, and there are rumors going around that you have been fired, or sick, or something. PPPLLLLEEEEAAAASSSSSEEEEEE let me know whats happening, the sub is nice but nowhere near good enough, I need an ▇▇ reccomendation, everyone wants to skip from now on, etc etc. anyway email me back, or even just call my house ▇▇▇▇▇▇ Thanks, and if you got fired rest assured we WILL raise hell, ▇▇▇▇▇ and the entire ▇▇▇▇▇ student body. Oh and ▇▇▇ pissed too

WILL CRIMINAL CHARGES BE FILED?

The decision to file criminal charges or prosecute is made by local law enforcement and/or the Commonwealth's Attorney.

Date	Time	Type of Interaction	Name(s)
December	5:00 pm	VICTIM INTERVIEW	Caine Blaise

StatusCompleted   Location   Face to Face(Other)

Taped Yes   Reason Not Taped   Unfounded Summary ☐

Other(s) Present During Interview

Detective Addah , Police Dept.

Documentation

███ stated that he did not have a relationship with Ms. ███. ███ stated that he met her last year at school during second quarter. ███ stated that she was his best friend's (███ .) teacher. ███ stated that they hung out at school during flex time. ███ stated that Ms. ███ was ok. ███ did not want to talk anymore without a lawyer.

Date	Time	Type of Interaction	Name(s)
December		CARETAKER INTERVIEW	Willow Kincaid

StatusCompleted   Location   Letter

Taped No   Reason Not Taped   Unfounded Summary ☐

Other(s) Present During Interview

Documentation

Certified letter # ████████████ sent to Ms. Reid indicating that an investigation was in progress and to contact worker.

Date	Time	Type of Interaction	Name(s)
January		CARETAKER INTERVIEW	Willow Kincaid

StatusCompleted   Location   Other

Taped No   Reason Not Taped   Unfounded Summary ☐

Other(s) Present During Interview

Documentation   Kincaid   Kincaid

Mr. O'Hanlon (attorney for Ms. ███. stated that Ms. ███ has been advised by counsel not to speak with CPS.

Date	Time	Type of Interaction	Name(s)
January		CONTACT	Ray O'Hanlon Attorney for Ms. Reid in the civil case.

Type/Location Fax   Status Completed

Purpose

Case Consultation

Information/Referral

Comments   Kincaid

Letter informed worker that Mr. O'Hanlon was representing Ms. ███. Letter also requested CPS file.

So at the end of all this . . . (See next document), CPS decided the allegations were, " . . . unfounded due to lack of evidence." After three months of hell, CPS concluded that there was no evidence because, " . . . Caine stated in an interview that he and Ms. Kincaid did not have a relationship." Wait, wasn't that interview back in December?

Date	Time	Type of Interaction	Name(s)
January		CONTACT	Ray O'Hanlon Attorney for Ms. Kincaid in the civil case.

Type/Location Letter   Status Completed

Purpose
   Case Consultation
   Information/Referral

Comments
   Letter informed worker that Mr. O'Hanlon was representing Ms Kincaid Letter also requested CPS file.

Date	Time	Type of Interaction	Name(s)
February		NEEDS ASSESSMENT	Caine Blaise

Needs   Strengths
No Needs

Services Needed

Type	Provided By	Status	Court
			No

Comments

Date	Time	Type of Interaction	Name(s)
March		FINDINGS	Caine Blaise

Disposition Unfounded - lack of evidence   Alleged A/N Willow Kincaid
A/N Catg   Sexual Abuse   A/N Type
VAC   Word Doc

Dispositional Assessment:

Other Services Provided:

Unfounded Summary
   The disposition is unfounded due to lack of evidence. Caine stated in an interview that he and Ms. Kincaid did not have a relationship. Ms. K... was advised by her lawyer not to speak w/ CPS.

Oh, yes, the other part of the **Unfounded Summary** is, "Ms. Kincaid was advised by her lawyer not to speak w/CPS." I can't even envision the alternate reality in which I would have refuted Caine's statement.

I think the rest is self-explanatory.

March

RE: Ms. Willow Kincaid, Child Protective Services Investigator

Dear ████████

We have responded to the child abuse/neglect report made on December concerning Caine Blaise. A thorough investigation was completed. After meeting with all concerned parties, we have determined these allegations to be UNFOUNDED. No further action can be taken at this time.

Thank you for taking the time to make this report; your concern is appreciated. If you have any questions or concerns about this assessment, please feel free to contact me at

Sincerely /

Child Protective Services

Re: Willow Kincaid   CPS Unfounded Determination

Dear   CPS

I have been retained by Ms. Kincaid to represent her in connection with the above-referenced "UNFOUNDED" determination. By way of this letter, Ms Kincaid respectfully requests that CPS promptly provide to the undersigned a copy of all information contained in CPS's file relating to this matter. See Code #) (providing that "[t]he subject of the complaint or report shall have access to [her] own record"). In addition, Ms. Kincaid respectfully requests that CPS provide the undersigned with a summary of its investigation and an explanation of how the information gathered supports the disposition. See Code ████ ██ (4) (requiring CPS to submit to the alleged abuser written notification of the findings and providing that "[t]hat notification shall include a summary of the investigation and an explanation of how the information gathered supports the disposition. [Emphasis supplied.]").

We thank you in advance for your cooperation. Please call me if you have questions or wish to discuss this matter.

Sincerely,

Raymond O'Hanlon

After conducting a through investigation, it has been determined, that this allegation is unfounded. A confidential record will be kept on file by the local department of Child Protective Services for a period of one year. The subject of this investigation may request, in writing, to have the local department keep the record for an additional period of time, up to two years. The subject of this investigation may also submit, in writing, a request to review information about he or she contained in this record.

In accordance with the Code . . ✗. . . . . . . (enclosed) any person who is the subject of an unfounded investigation, that believes the complaint was made in bad faith or with malicious intent, may petition the court to obtain the identity of the complainant. This information may not be available if the complaint was made anonymously.

Thank you for your cooperation throughout this investigation, if you have any further questions or concerns, please contact me at _____ ▌

Sincerely▌

Child Protective Services.

Re: CPS Investigation File

Dear Willow

Enclosed for your information and files is a copy of CPS's investigation file. Please call me if you have questions or wish to discuss this matter. I hope all is well.

Sincerely, *signature*
Raymond O'Hanlon

RE: Willow Kincaid

Mr. O'Hanlon

In response to your letter to _____ CPS _____ enclosed please find a copy of the CPS file on your client, Willow Kincaid CPS is out of the office this week, upon his return he will provide you with the summary of investigation you requested.

If you have any questions or need further assistance, you may contact me at (.) -

Sincerely,

Social Services

So, you might think (as I did) that the whole incredibly destructive ordeal is over at this point. Ray called me with the news before I ever got my copy of the letter.

Just like my grandmother remembers VJ Day or my mother's generation knows where he/she was when Kennedy was shot or Generation X recalls the Challenger Disaster or how every person alive today knows incredible details of that moment on September 11, 2001, I'll never forget exactly where I was suspended in time when Ray said, "CPS came back with an 'unfounded' determination."

Even as he was speaking beyond the word "unfounded," my mind was busy with reparations. I thought about how the AP exam was a little over a month away; I wondered how much my substitute had covered, how much my kids needed. I anticipated being able to talk on my phone again, use email, IM, reconnect to the world. Maybe I could now drive without always wondering if I was being followed. Maybe I could reset my interior dome so that it would come on when I opened my car door.

More than anything else, I thought, "my poor baby, thank god it's over," but then I heard Ray's voice through my jubilant, jumbled brain. He was saying . . .

"Willow, I know it seems like good news . . . and it IS in a way, but it's not over."

I don't remember all the caveats he provided to a determination I felt should have been etched for eternity. All I can say at this juncture is my attorney was correct. It was far from over. After that day in March, when I got the good news . . . I don't even know how to concisely express what transpired. All I know is, after that, I deteriorated beyond recognition.

I promise you that the tale of events following my "unfounded" determination is a completely separate story, and my promise means so much that I've written all of that in *Tragic Hero: A Teacher Accused (TWO)*.

Before I sign out of this segment forever, I'm leaving you a final graphic. Some of you probably already have figured out the truth . . . or at least have a speculation, but if you feel unsatisfied at this conclusion, let me make the law very clear.

My case is not closed. There is no statute of limitations on my charges. I'm taking a risk putting what you have in your hands out there.

So, give me a break, please. I wouldn't be using money I don't have to produce this work if I didn't think it was of vast importance in the global scheme. I promise if you ride it out with me, you will be satisfied (albeit incensed) in the end.

Nightmare Before July
(that last question)

Knowing what you know now?

Everyone has an excuse for what is deemed unacceptable. It seems so arbitrary that all of a sudden at 18 humans can be held accountable for any and everything. How did that get to be the magic number?

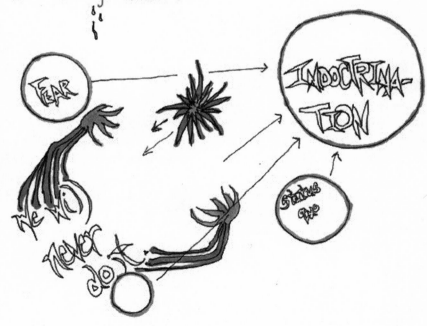

Re—read the **"Read This"** section of this book, and ask yourself again . . .